Melanie Graham

Whitecap Books
Vancouver/Toronto

Edited by Elaine Jones
Cover photographs by Bill Lewis
Cover design by Warren Clarke
Interior design by Carolyn Deby
Interior illustration by Melanie Graham

Typeset by The Vancouver Desktop Publishing Centre Ltd.

Printed and bound in Canada by D.W. Friesen and Sons Ltd.

Canadian Cataloguing in Publication Data

Graham, Melanie
  Short kutz

Includes index
ISBN 1-895099-91-9

1. Clothing and dress—Remaking. I. Title.
TT550.G72 1991   646.4′06   C91-091472-9

Dedicated to
the jubilation of Bryan
and the dreams of Elizabeth

CONTENTS

Introduction

The seeds for *Short Kutz* were planted a long time ago.

Once upon a time, my mother and my paternal grandmother taught me to sew. It was love at first stitch. I thought sewing machines were the most marvelous invention and fabric stores a kind of heaven.

My grandmother, to my knowledge, never used a pattern or a sewing machine. Yet some of the most beautiful nightgowns, dresses and doll clothes were produced by her patient and capable hands.

My mother made most of our clothes when we were little and managed to put imagination and love into every garment. I can still remember two dresses in particular; a little yellow sun dress with tiny white dots and elastic smocking that I wore when I was about three, and a beautiful, teal blue, cozy, winter dress that I wore around four. The blue dress was hand-smocked with rust-coloured thread and I wish I still had it.

By the time I was exposed to Home Economics in the seventh grade, there was no hope for me as a conventional seamstress. I failed Home Economics but have made most of my own and my children's clothes ever since.

The next step towards *Short Kutz* came about when I became involved in the operation of an outdoor clothing factory. Over an eight-year period I learned to make and grade patterns and helped to solve countless design problems. Working with professional seamstresses introduced production-style sewing to my own sewing room. In that same time period I gave birth to four beautiful but ever-growing children. So there I was, with no time to spare, children to dress, a tight budget and a warehouse of zippers, buckles, ribbed cuffing and bright fabric scraps around me every day. The only possible outcome was *Short Kutz*. But I wasn't there yet.

Short Kutz is a blending of the traditional practice of cutting down adult clothes for children and the more contemporary skill of commercial patternmaking. I never thought to formalize and teach the concept until someone asked me to run a short course for their store. To teach a course, you need to have some information down on paper. This works best with a title or name of some kind and that's what finally led to *Short Kutz*.

Short Kutz has evolved considerably since I taught that first class. At first it was just something I did for fun. Then I saw the effect it had on the people I taught. They didn't just have fun, they absorbed the concept and took off with it! In the last two years I've seen one woman use it to create a snowsuit for her daughter; I only taught her to work with denim or corduroy. Two other women placed first and second in our local craft fair with it. I had thought of entering the same fair, but now I'm glad I didn't. They sew better than I do with my own idea! On several occasions people have taken the course and phoned a few days later in great excitement. They were being paid to make more clothes based on the same concept! I've received letters from people as far away as Ontario and New Brunswick who saw some of the finished garments and wanted to learn how to make them.

So what exactly is *Short Kutz*? It's a new sewing system that's applicable to as wide a range of raw materials as your budget, your closet and your imagination will produce. Every project in *Short Kutz* uses a set of guides, or curves, with detailed instructions for the production of a range of related or similar garments. The guides can be applied directly to used clothing or laid out on paper to produce a wide variety of sewing patterns. You will find no guides or "pattern pieces" for things like collars, cuffs, facings or interfacings. You will, however, find instructions for making whatever is necessary to complete the garment or garments pictured in the unit. There is a chapter of detailed instruction for each of nine different types of outfits, with the tenth chapter devoted to customizing the guides and developing the patterns that are applied throughout the book. The patterns in Chapter 10 are not restricted to use with recycled clothing, however, but can be easily and quickly applied to new fabric as well.

At the very back of the book you will find a family size chart. This is to make measuring easier, but it can also personalize a gift of the book if you fill the chart out with the measurements for someone special to the recipient of the book.

You can work with a *Short Kutz* unit to produce as many sizes of any garment as you wish. Properly applied, Short Kutz will give you the know-how to create custom clothing for anyone; to become a fashion designer! Every unit goes beyond basic instructions to include many ideas for varying the finished product, but these are just suggestions. Your own imagination and selection of used clothing will provide even more inspiration.

Short Kutz was designed by a parent, for parents. It's a system that allows you to cut corners and costs. Even a beginning seamstress can use this system.

Short Kutz is also an excellent way to put a lot of the *stuff* you thought you'd never use to good use. If a sock top still has enough snap left to its ribbing, or if old underwear have even a few inches of functional elastic left, you can use them. *Short Kutz* will help you to look at all your potential castoffs in a new light. With a little practice you'll eventually find a use for almost anything.

Another unexpected plus for many folks

first trying *Short Kutz* has been an increase in confidence and enthusiasm for all their sewing projects. When you're busy raising a family and often working part or full time, it gets harder and harder to finish all the sewing projects that you've cut out and partially assembled. The bigger your backlog of half done clothing gets the more discouraged you get. Before you know it, you've quit sewing altogether. This changes when you find you can finish something in the same evening or afternoon that you started it.

Finally, *Short Kutz* is fun. There's no apprehension involved when you hack up an old pair of jeans. Remember how you felt the first time you worked with fabric that cost more than $15 a metre? That first cut almost made your heart stop. *Short Kutz* gives you the freedom to let your hair down a little and really experiment. Your finished product can be as sophisticated or off the wall as you want it to be.

Short Kutz will never be finished. Everyone who learns this system adds to it. In the past two years I've learned from all the people I've taught and tried to pass their good ideas on to the next class. Right now *Short Kutz* touches on many contemporary issues. It's economical, so in that regard it will always be an issue. It's also an easy step towards caring about the environment. Not only does it help you to recycle, but it also helps you to consume locally, buying from within your own community. (The big tag for that one is bioregionalism.) This puts fewer trucks on the freeways bringing you products they made in another community and redirects your cash flow back into your own neighbourhood. All good ideas.

My favorite part of *Short Kutz* is what it does for you, the you that's inside, buried under reality. Reality is all the stuff necessary for survival, the mountain of little chores that keeps you from finding time to know and be yourself. Creativity and the chance to accomplish something you're proud of are critical to the health of your spirit. If your spirit smiles, you do good things in this world. I believe that learning to make something out of nothing, especially in a short time period, helps you to become a stronger and more positive human being.

Wind your bobbins, oil your machines, haul the Good Will bag out of the front closet and have a ball. Remember, nice as it is to save money and do good things for your kids, you deserve a little fun once in a while. With *Short Kutz*, you can have it all.

So welcome to *Short Kutz*. May you create it and wear it in the finest of health. It won't cut the grass or dice and slice vegetables for you. It won't balance your books or help you to lose weight overnight. It's just fun, economical and environmentally sound. But that's not bad either.

CHAPTER ONE

Jeans to Overalls

Designing and making children's overalls from adult pants

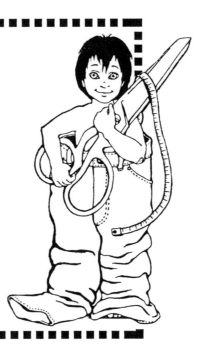

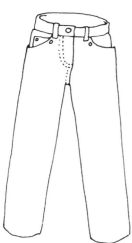 +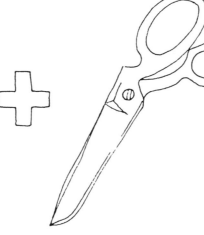

=

1. Measure

1. Measure your child (or someone else's) according to the diagram.

2. Measure the circumference of the adult garment at midthigh, then double this measurement. Now subtract 28 cm (11 inches). If the resulting figure is the same as or smaller than the child's hips, then the adult garment is too narrow. Try a larger pair of jeans or refer to NOTES for suggestions. If it's larger than the child's hips, then carry on.

3. Select a length of facing fabric at least 26 cm (10 inches) wide and longer than the doubled thigh measurement.

4. Measure the leg length of the adult garment and compare it to the sum of the child's front body length and inseam. If the adult jeans are longer than the child, make the overalls. The jean tops can be used to make a jacket, vest or bag. If the legs of the adult jeans are shorter than the child's inseam and body measurement, make short overalls or, once again, refer to NOTES for suggestions.

5. Measure and cut two lengths of 2.5-cm (1-inch) elastic for shoulder straps. Remember to add 10 cm (4 inches) to the shoulder strap measurement. Cut one end of each strap with a 45-degree angle. This will make it easier to apply them at the right angle when you sew them into the overalls.

(Measure your patience if your child is helping. Measure your sanity if several children are helping.)

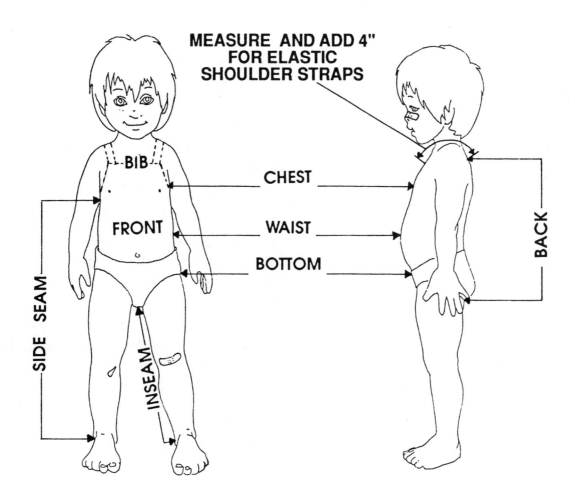

MEASURE AND ADD 4"
FOR ELASTIC
SHOULDER STRAPS

BIB

CHEST

FRONT

WAIST

BOTTOM

BACK

SIDE SEAM

INSEAM

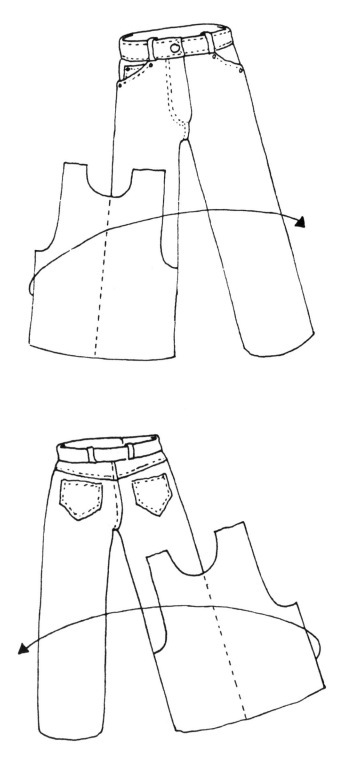

2. Mark

You can buy dressmaker's chalk or washable markers to mark your garment, but an ordinary, washable pencil works fine too.

✂ **IF YOU'VE MADE A PATTERN** *(see page 113)*

1. Place the inseam of the BACK HALF of the pattern against the front inseam of the adult pant leg. Be sure to place the bottom edge of the pattern at the bottom edge of the jean cuff. If you're going to be applying ribbed cuffing to the overalls, cut the hems off the adult pants before applying the pattern.

The long line coming up from the crotch curve should run parallel to the inseam of the adult pants leg. Make sure, also, that the adult pants leg is wide enough to extend to the middle of the pattern. To make this easier to see, you may want to drop a line straight down from the centre of the armpit to the centre of the bottom edge of the leg. This line would represent the side seam in a conventional pair of overalls.

2. Trace the outline of the pattern on the jeans.

3. Flip the pattern and repeat the process for the other leg of the adult pants.

4. Turn the adult pants over and smooth them out again, making sure that the inseam mark on the front is visible from the back.

5. Place the inseam of the FRONT HALF of your pattern on the inseam of the adult pants leg. Make sure that this inseam point matches the one already marked on the front of the adult pant leg. Once again, keep the long line sweeping up from the crotch parallel to the side seam of the adult pants.

If the jeans you're working with have a blown knee, simply rotate the leg of the jeans until the tear or hole is on the edge before placing the pattern. Remember to rotate the other leg of the adult jeans the same amount so that both sides of the finished overalls will match.

6. Trace the pattern on the adult pant leg.

7. Flip the pattern and repeat the process on the other pant leg.

8. Check to be sure that your inseam points are all at the same height, then check that all the armpit curves line up as well. It's essential that all the inseam points line up, but if there is a slight difference in the armpit lines, just draw in a new line that evens things out.

Once you are sure that your work is as similar as possible to the illustration (if not better) you are ready to get out the scissors.

Remember to cut a *single thickness only*. Each leg of the adult garment will be one half of the completed overalls.

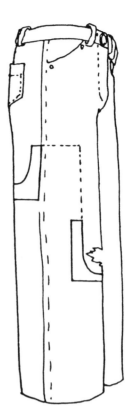

✂ IF YOU HAVEN'T MADE A PATTERN

Select guides **A**, and **B**, **C** and **D**.

1. Measure up the inside leg seam and mark the child's inseam length. If you're applying cuffs to the overalls, measure the inseam after you've cut the hem off the adult pants.

2. Place front crotch guide **B** at this point, as shown, and draw the curve (not the right-angled corner).

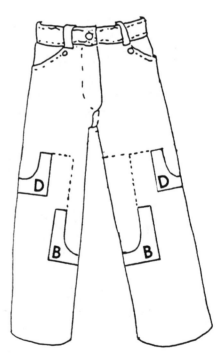

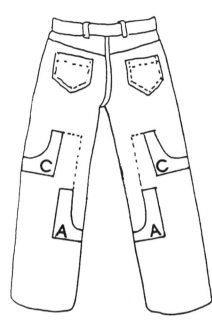

3. Flip the guide and do the same for the other leg of the adult jeans.

4. In the event that the adult jeans have a blown knee, simply rotate the leg until the hole is on the edge. Make sure that both legs are rotated the same amount, in the same direction, then place your guides.

5. From the inseam mark, measure up the child's front length and mark it. This time, place armpit guide **D** at the top of the line but on the outside seam of the adult pant. Do the same on the other leg.

6. Flip the jeans and repeat steps 1 through 5, using the back guides **A** and **C** as shown. When laid out now, the marks for guides **A** and **B** should line up, as should those for **C** and **D**.

7. Now cut on the lines you've marked, *single thickness only*.

3. Make

By now the phone is ringing, the baby needs nursing and a two-year-old is balancing your chequebook.

1. Take what's left of the jeans and a seam picker and liberate a back pocket for the overalls bib while you finish your coffee.

2. Take each half of the cut overalls and place them, right sides together, on a single thickness of facing fabric. Make sure that the facing fabric extends down the same length on each half of the overalls. If the facing fabric is new cotton material, wash and dry it before using it. The pants you're working with are preshrunk, so the lining or facing should be too, otherwise the finished product will pucker badly after the first wash.

3. Trace and cut the facings.

4. Sew the facings together at the bib front

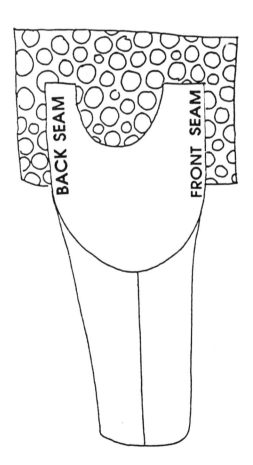

and bib back, being sure to keep the right sides of the fabric together.

5. Take one-half of the overalls and turn it inside out. Now stick the right-side-out half of the overalls inside the other half, right sides together.

6. Be sure the inseams match and that you have the front to the front and the back to the back.

(If you've done everything right and you have a front to a back, then you've cut out two left halves or two right halves! Don't despair . . . find another pair of jeans and cut out two of whatever you're missing and have two pairs of two-tone overalls!)

7. Now sew the crotch seam before the baby wakes up. Then turn the overalls right side out. See, you're almost done!

8. Hem or serge the bottom edge of the facing, then pin it, right sides together, to the overalls.

9. Insert the elastic shoulder straps between the facing and the overalls, at the top edge of the back bib, with the straps hanging down the back of the overalls.

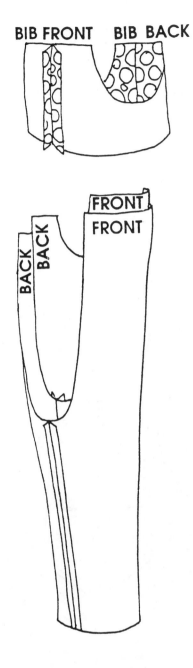

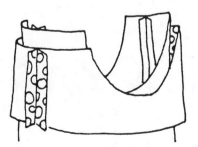

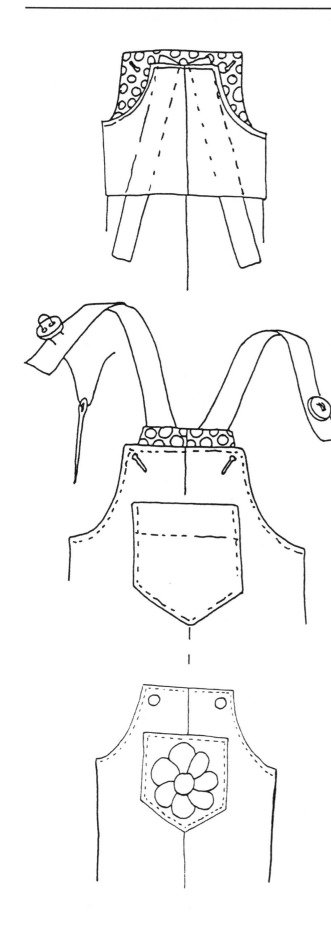

10. If you have cut one end of each elastic at a 45-degree angle, place the points of the angled ends of the shoulder straps at the centre seam so that the straps angle out a bit, then pin them in place.

11. Sew the facing to the overalls with at least a double line of stitching over the shoulder elastics. Be careful not to catch any other part of the straps while attaching the facing.

12. Clip your corners and your curves, especially if you work with a generous seam allowance. If you're using a serger you may want to check that you didn't miss any stitches when sewing in the shoulder straps.

13. Turn the facing to the inside of the garment. Be sure that the corners of the bibs are completely turned. Long nails are good for this, or a dull pencil.

14. Topstitch the top edge of the overalls. This will help the finished garment to hang right. A long stitch running about .5 cm (¼ inch) in from the edge usually works best. If you have a fancier machine, this would be a good place to apply a double needle stitch or an embroidery stitch.

And we're coming in on the home stretch.

15. Lightly pin, then sew on the pocket or pockets you picked off earlier, being careful to keep the facing smooth and in line with the overalls (whenever the facing extends down far enough to be caught in the stitch line of the pocket).

16. Put buttonholes in the top corners of the front bib, unless of course you have chosen to use snaps.

17. Try the garment on your child and mark the straps for the right placement of the snaps or buttons.

18. If you're using snaps you may want to put an extra snap on each shoulder strap to allow for growth. If you are planning, expecting or already have younger children, add a third snap on each strap to accommodate the smaller size.

19. Unless you have an unusually placid child, it's recommended that you remove the overalls before sewing on the buttons. (Resist the urge, even if you've had a really bad day.)

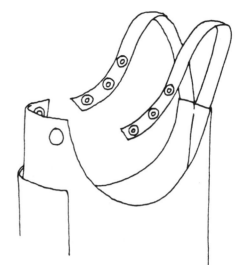

4. Notes

Adult Jeans Too Narrow

1. In the event that the jeans you have selected are too narrow, don't despair. When you choose your facing fabric, choose one that is fairly rugged and cut two strips, each 8 to 10 cm (3 or 4 inches) wide and the same length as the overall side seam. You can either pick out the existing side seam or cut it out altogether. Just be sure to do the same thing on both sides or you'll end up with lopsided pants.

2. Now sew your fabric strips in, being sure to keep right sides together.

3. When you have completed this extra step, return to step one of the MAKE part of these instructions.

4. If you have a serger, you may want to try a tough rib-knit fabric for an action insert, with more of the same rib-knit for stretch cuffs.

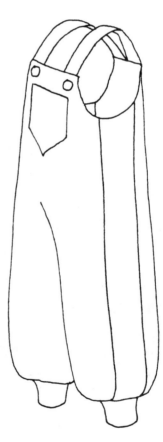

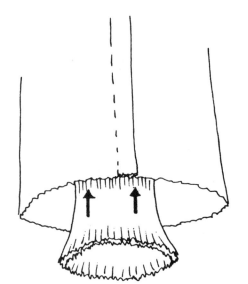

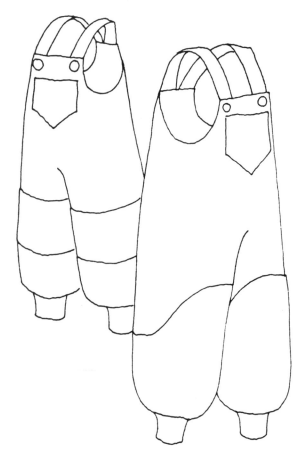

5. If you have no cuffing, let alone lengths of rib-knit, but you do have a serger, try the cuffs from an old sweater and use lengths of the sweater body for your stretch inserts.

6. If a stretch insert is your choice, then cut your facing to match the overalls, not the stretch panel.

Adult Jeans Too Short

If the adult jeans are too short and you don't want short overalls, there are a few options open to you.

1. Throw the adult jeans in a box in the basement, sell your sewing machine and go to the nearest bargain basement to buy a pair of overalls.

2. If the overalls are just a little too short, pick out the hem and sew on elastic cuffing. To do this you merely turn the pant leg inside out, stick the cuff, right end first, into the pant leg and sew it on. Be sure to stretch the cuffing to fit the pant leg as you sew it on.

3. If you have no cuffing, hate cuffing or had something else in mind, check an upholstery store for some long strips of tough, bright remnants. Cut the finished overalls off at the knees and use the heavy fabric to make an insert for each leg. Be sure to make both inserts the same depth and the same circumference as the pant leg. Also, remember to adjust the overall pant leg length to fit your child. If the knee inserts are made of really tough fabric, you may want to line them with matching strips from an old flannelette sheet before you attach the inserts to the overall legs.

You could use more of the same bright remnant for facing, pockets, appliqués . . . even gathered covers for the elastic shoulder straps. If you're really lucky you may even have enough for a shirt.

4. A variation on knee inserts is to replace the whole bottom half of the pant leg with some rugged, possibly waterproof, material that suits your fancy or sits idle in your scrap box.

Adult Jeans Too Wide

1. If the adult pants are too wide for your child, you can set the crotch guide in from the adult inseam and drop a line straight down to the hem. (This means you have to sew the inseam on the child's pants before assembly.) In this case it's a good idea to either cut off the original hem of the jeans or unpick a section of them before sewing the new inseam; otherwise you end up with a bulky lump in the hem right at the child's inner ankle.

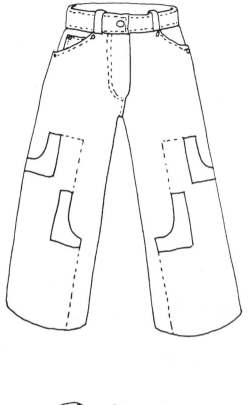

Suggestions

1. For extra-special overalls, open the inseam before sewing the garment. This makes it easier to put on fancy pockets, knee patches, appliqué—whatever your imagination can contrive! It also means you can apply snaps to the inseam for easy access to a child in diapers.

2. You don't want to do any hemming if you can possibly avoid it! Use what's there, including all the finished details of the adult garment—pockets, hems, zips, buttons, labels.

3. Lining the pocket to match the facing adds colour—so does a zipper in the pocket, or lace around the bib! Dig through your scrap box, add beads, buttons, anything you want. Just remember . . . have fun!

CHAPTER TWO

Jeans to Jackets

Designing and
making
children's
jackets and
vests from
adult pants

(This information can be used to make adult-sized vests and jackets as well)

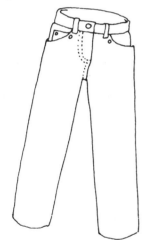 + 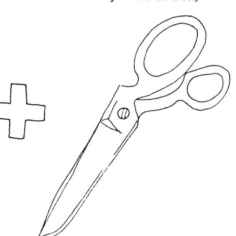 =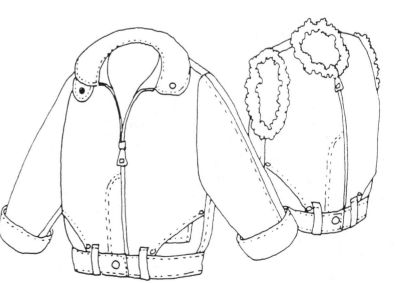

1. Measure

1. Measure your child as shown. If your child is under three, you may want to take a break after measuring!

2. Measure the adult garment to be sure that the waist is large enough to accommodate your child's hips. If the pants waist is not large enough for your child's hips, then you will have to find a larger pair of pants. If it's too big, please refer to **NOTES**.

3. The adult pants must also be long enough to accommodate your child's full body length and sleeve length combined. If they're longer than you need, just save the scraps for imaginative pockets or patches. If the adult pants are too short for your child's jacket, please refer to **NOTES**.

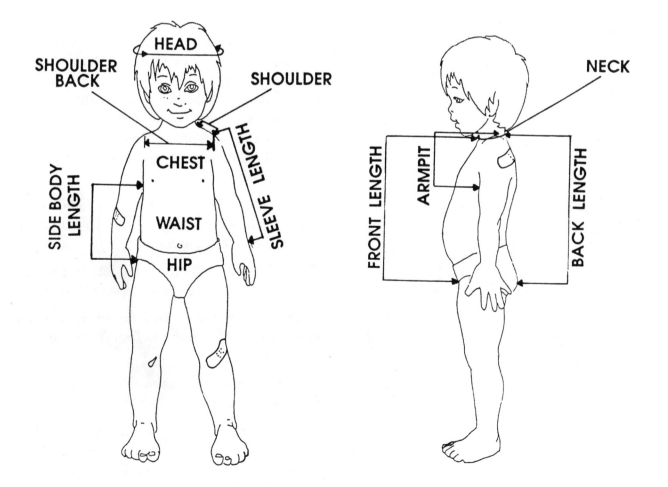

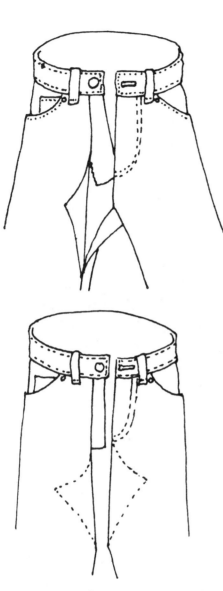

2. Mark

Dressmaker's chalk or washable markers work well, but any washable pencil works fine too. Before you mark the adult jeans at all, however, it's necessary to do a little bit of seam picking.

✂ PREPARING THE ADULT JEANS

1. You need to remove the zipper in the fly but hang on to the flap that lies behind the fly. You'll need it when you put in your new zipper.

2. Continue to open the crotch seam all the way around through the curve of the seat.

3. Open the inseam of both thighs, at least 30 cm (12 inches) along from the crotch.

4. Lay the jeans flat on your work surface, face up.

5. The fold of the front fly of the pants is a straight line, but the crotch seam that you just picked open curves to point before it curves back to join the straight line of the pant leg. Open up the folded edge of the seam at the base of the fly and refold the original seam so that the crotch point is folded right back.

6. This should create a straight folded edge that extends from the original fly fold to join the fold of the leg seam.

7. If necessary, pin this new fold in place, or even iron it, if you prefer to sew that way.

8. Do the same for both sides of the front fly, being careful to save the flap from the original fly.

9. Now turn the pants over and smooth them flat again.

10. The seat of a pair of pants is fairly flat before it begins to curve into the crotch. The seam must be picked open to this point.

11. If the pants have a plain seam, merely sew a new seam that continues the straight line of the flat part of the back of the pants.

12. When you have sewn this seam to your satisfaction, high enough to include your child's back body length, then you may cut off the old crotch curve. But you don't have to.

13. If the adult pants have a flat-felled seam, return to the jeans lying face down, flat on your work surface.

14. With a flat-felled seam, one piece of fabric very obviously lies on top of the other. Smooth out the pants back with the upper crotch lying flat pointing in one direction while the underneath crotch points flat in the other direction.

15. Make sure you have created a flat back that is high enough to accommodate your child's back body measurement, then pin the fabric in place, keeping the edges rolled under to match the original seam.

16. To sew this, follow the stitch lines from the still-remaining flat-felled seam and continue them up through the curve you have laid flat on the back.

Now you're ready to mark the jeans for cutting.

✂ IF YOU'VE MADE A PATTERN *(see page 116)*

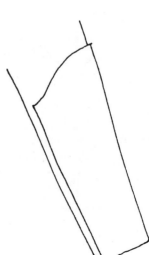

1. Place the sleeve pattern on the leg of the adult jeans, with the longer straight edge along the fancier seam of the pant leg. The wrist of the pattern piece should lie flush with the hem of the pant leg.

2. Trace the shoulder curve and cut the pant leg off along this line.

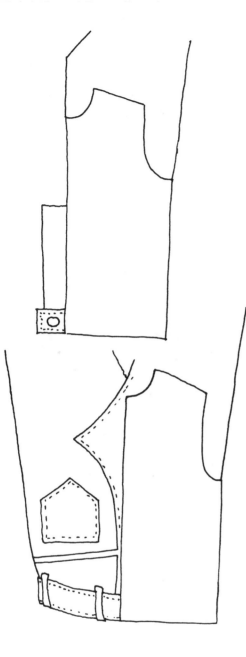

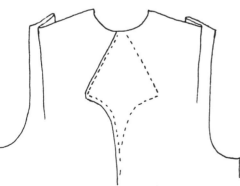

3. If the pant leg is much wider than the pattern, trace both the shoulder curve and the underarm seam of the pattern on the pant leg. In this case you will have to add 2.5 cm (1 inch) of seam allowance when you draw the underarm seam, as you will be cutting the sleeve open along this line.

4. Use the sleeve you've just cut out as a pattern for the other sleeve by flipping it over and placing it on the other pant leg. Be sure that both legs are folded the same way and lined up carefully at the cuffs before you cut out the second sleeve.

5. Open up the rest of the pants inseam so that you can lay the upper part of the adult jeans out flat.

6. Place the jacket front pattern piece on one side of the pants front, lining up the waistband of the pattern with the waistband of the adult jeans. Keep the straight front edge of the pattern piece flush with the folded front edge of the adult jeans.

7. Trace the pattern.

8. Lay the adult jeans out flat, right side up, and place the pattern back on the jeans back. Be careful to line up the centre line of the pattern with the centre of the jeans back and the pattern waistband with the waistband of the adult jeans.

9. Trace the half of the pattern that is on the same side as the front that you've already marked. If the underarms don't quite match up, bring the higher line down to match the lower line. If the adult jeans turn out to be far too wide for the pattern, simply extend the shoulder lines so that the pattern pieces can be reapplied at the side seams. When you sew the garment later, pleat the shoulders to achieve the correct size.

10. Before cutting, fold the adult jeans precisely in half along the centre back line. Be extremely careful to line up the waistband, front folds and side seams. Pin them in place just to be on the safe side, otherwise you may find the material shifts out of line when you try to cut it, double thickness.

11. Be careful not to cut straight across from one shoulder seam to the other. You may be cutting your collar too small. The U-shaped piece created by cutting out the armpit must be measured along the seam at its centre and cut off at half of the neck measurement. (Refer to step 15 of MARK without using a pattern.)

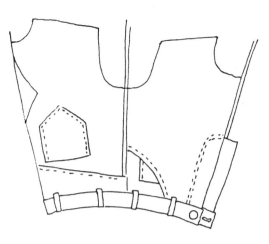

✂ IF YOU HAVEN'T MADE A PATTERN

Select guides **E**, **F** and **G**.

1. If you wish to put ribbed cuffs on the jacket, cut off the hems of the adult jeans (or pick them out).

2. From the hem, measure up the side seams of the adult pant leg the desired sleeve length and place sleeve guide **F** at this point. Be sure to keep the shoulder point to the side seam and the armpit point to the inseam. Trace the guide.

3. Flip the guide to do the other leg; otherwise you will end up with two left or two right sleeves.

4. Cut the sleeves, *double thickness.*

5. Measure the child's jacket front length up the centre of the jeans front from the waistband and place front neck guide **E** at this point, first on one side, then the other. Be careful to lay the centre line of the guide along the edge of the centre fold of the jeans front.

6. Trace the guide.

7. Measure up the sides of the adult jeans to achieve the jacket side length, and place

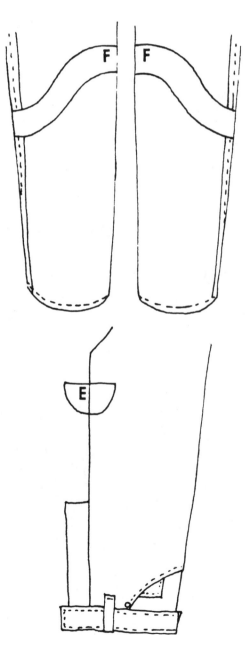

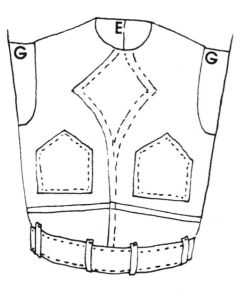

armpit guide **G** at this point as shown, first on one side, then the other.

8. Draw a line from the top of the armpit to the top edge of the neck to creat the shoulder seam line. Make sure the shoulder lengths match each other and your child's shoulder measurement.

9. If the shoulder line is far too large, merely stick in a pleat, or angle armpit guide **G** to achieve the desired shoulder length. Be sure to do the same for both sides.

10. Flip the adult jeans and measure the child's back body length up the centre. Place back neck guide **E** at this point. All going well, it should be a little higher than the front neck.

11. Trace the guide.

12. From the front of the jeans, extend the marks for the bottom point of the armpits around so you can see them from the back, and once again place the bottom of armpit guide **G** at this point.

13. Extend a line from the neck curve out and down slightly to mark the desired shoulder width (matching the front shoulder width, please).

14. Now angle the guide towards this shoulder point and trace it. If you have to angle the guide out more than 2.5 to 5 cm (1 to 2 inches), you will have to cut the back shoulder much wider than the front and then pleat it to match the front.

15. You should now have the jeans marked. A quick way to ensure that both sides of the jacket match is to fold the jeans in half along the centre back before cutting it out. Carefully line up the waistband, front fold lines and side seams. Pin them in place as the fabric tends to shift when you are cutting it. Now cut the jacket out, *double thickness*.

16. Be very careful when cutting out the jacket body not to cut straight across the armpit from the front to the back shoulder. You need this U-shaped piece of denim (or whatever fabric you are recycling) to make your collar.

17. Now take the neck measurement of your child and add 10 to 13 cm (4 or 5 inches). If it's too much you can always cut back later, but if it's too small, you can't stretch it.

18. Measure along the straightest edge of the U-shaped pieces you've saved from cutting the armpit and cut them off at half of this enlarged neck measurement. If you cut straight across you will get a close fitting collar, but if you angle the cut out from the straight edge you've measured you'll get a more open effect.

19. Now make sure the U-shaped pieces match one another.

20. Sew the two pieces together at the straight edge you just cut and there you have your collar!

If the kids are playing quietly, sleeping or at school, now might be a good time for a peaceful cup of tea or coffee.

3. Make

The Lining

1. Lay your lining fabric out on your cutting surface, single thickness, and lay the jacket body out smoothly (right sides together). The jacket body will lie in a gentle curve, so don't worry about keeping too closely to the grain of the fabric or matching up plaids or stripes. It just isn't possible.

It isn't always necessary to buy new fabric for a jacket lining. Check your cupboards for old quilts, blankets or sleeping bags. (No down though please!)

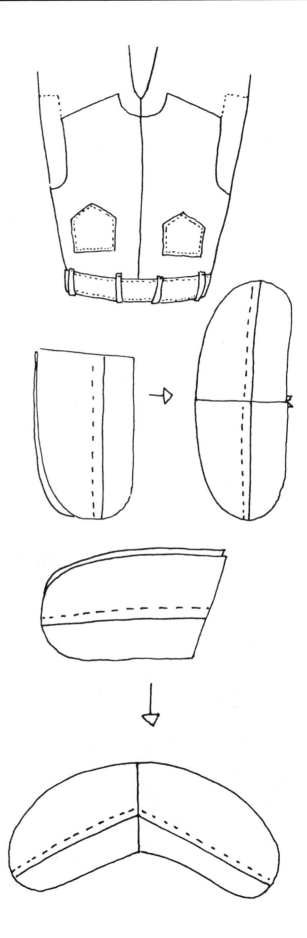

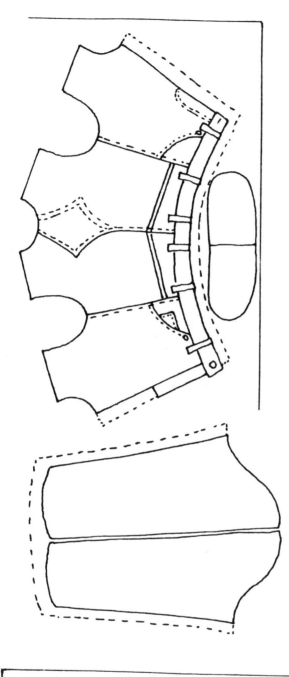

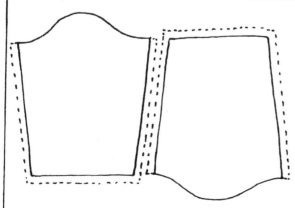

2. Trace the jacket body on the lining, giving yourself at least a 2-cm (3/4-inch) seam allowance wherever the jacket has a finished edge (e.g. waistband, front opening, end of sleeves, etc.). If the adult garment has an elasticized waistband, stretch it out to mark it. An extra set of hands or a knee helps here.

3. If the jacket body has belt loops, extend the lining beyond the edge of the waistband. If there are no belt loops, you may prefer to finish the lining at the top edge of the waistband. This makes for a less bulky waistband.

4. Place the sleeve set on the lining together, back to back, lined up at the shoulder seams so that they look like one sleeve laid open.

5. Trace this single sleeve, allowing a seam allowance everywhere but at the shoulder.

6. Cut out the sleeve, flip the cut piece and use it to trace out the second sleeve.

7. Place the collar on the lining fabric, right sides together, trace it, and cut it out.

The Jacket

1. Before you start sewing your jacket together, you might want to attach any pockets, badges or other extras that you've decided to add on. It's a lot easier to do with the jacket laid out flat.

2. Sew the shoulder seams of the lining, right sides together.

3. Do the same for the jacket body. Be sure to sew the front shoulders to the back shoulders.

4. If you need to put pleats in at the shoulders, now's the time to do it. Remember to make both sides of the jacket the same (as in left and right sides). If you need to pleat both the front shoulders and the back, it looks most effective if you line up all your pleats right at the sleeve edge.

This way they work like an action pleat for the jacket.

5. Mark the centres of the armholes of the jacket lining and insert the sleeve linings, being careful to line up the midpoint of the armhole with the underarm seam of the sleeves. Be careful also to keep the right sides together. Pin the underarm half of the sleeve in first. Sew in the lining sleeves.

6. Repeat step 5 for the jacket.

7. Sometimes, when inserting the sleeves, you will find that they are a little large for the armhole. If this is the case, merely put a few gathers or pleats in at the shoulder of the sleeve and tell your friends that you planned it that way.

8. If the sleeve is too small for the armhole, check the dimensions of both and compare them to your desired armhole size. If the armhole is the right size you will have to cut or pick open the sleeve and sew in a strip of fabric (artfully of course) to widen it. If the armhole is too large, simply tighten it up a little at the shoulder by angling the shoulder seams down a little more steeply from the neck.

9. Insert the sleeves of the jacket, lining up the side seams in the jacket body with the underarm seams in the sleeves. Sew in the sleeves.

10. Turn the lining of the jacket inside out and insert it into the jacket to see if it fits.

The Zipper

1. Place your jacket zipper, right side up, behind the right-hand front edge of the jacket body. This is usually the side of the pants that has the flap from the original fly.

2. Place the zipper between the flap and the front folded edge of the jacket, lining up the back edge of the zipper with the back edge of the fly flap.

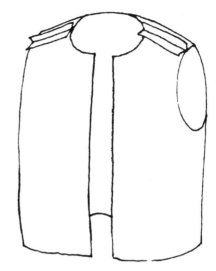

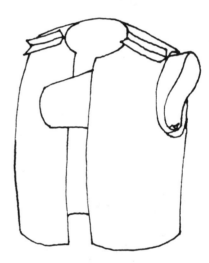

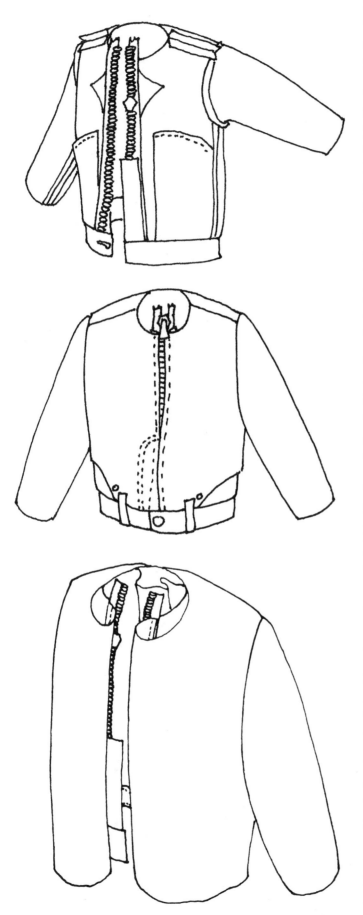

3. Sew it in place with the jacket right side up, being sure that the zipper extends from the top edge of the waistband to just beyond the neck line.

4. Unzip the zipper completely into two separate pieces. Place the bottom of the free piece at the waistband on the inside of the other 'left-hand' side of the jacket front. Make sure that the bottom point of the zipper is sitting on top of the stitch line from the original fly of the jeans.

5. At this point you may notice that the second half of the zipper sits well back from the front edge of the jacket. This is because you're dealing with a waistband designed around a fly-type zipper.

What you have to do now is angle the zipper out as you sew it in the rest of the way. Angle it so that it is flush with the folded front edge before it reaches the base of the old fly.

6. Once again, be sure the zipper extends a bit beyond the neck of the jacket.

7. Zip up the zipper and make sure that the neck edges match at the top. If they don't, mark the level of the lower neckline on the higher side. This is to enable you to sew the collar in with greater accuracy.

Attaching the Lining

1. Line up the top neck edges of your lining with the top neck edges of your jacket.

2. Place the front edge of the lining for each side of the jacket against the back side of the zipper, being sure that the right side of the lining is up against the back side of the zipper.

3. Keep the raw edge of the lining in line with the back edge of the zipper and sew it in place. You now have a double-stitched zipper too. To be on the safe side, you might want to run your stitching line back and forth a little at the bottom end of both sides of the zipper. This is a real stress point in a child's jacket and needs all the strength it can get.

4. Turn the jacket lining to the inside of the jacket now, being particularly careful to get the lining and jacket shoulder and underarm seams smoothly lined up. Don't sew it in though.

The Collar

1. Measure across the base of the collar, mark your child's neck measurement plus 7 to 10 cm (3 or 4 inches). Use the centre seam in the collar to centre this measurement.

2. Make a mark on the collar to show these two points.

3. If you wish to insert a strap or tab at one side of the collar, pin it in place 1.5 cm (½ inch) up from the bottom edge of the collar. Place it pointing in, between the right sides of the lining and collar.

4. With right sides together, sew the collar lining to the collar, leaving it open between the two points you marked a few minutes ago. It's a good idea to double your stitching over the base of the tab.

5. Turn the collar right side out. If you wish to, this would be a good time to press it flat, unless of course you are lining the jacket with polyester fleece or pile. It tends to melt when you try to press it.

6. Before you attach the collar, as mentioned earlier, zip the jacket up and check that both sides of the neck are the same height. If they don't match up, mark a point on the high side that matches the height of the lower neck edge.

I would suggest trimming the top edges of the neck to match, but then you would have to trim the zipper, and this doesn't leave you enough of a tail on the zipper to ensure that the slider won't slip right off the first time a child or teacher really pulls on it to do it up.

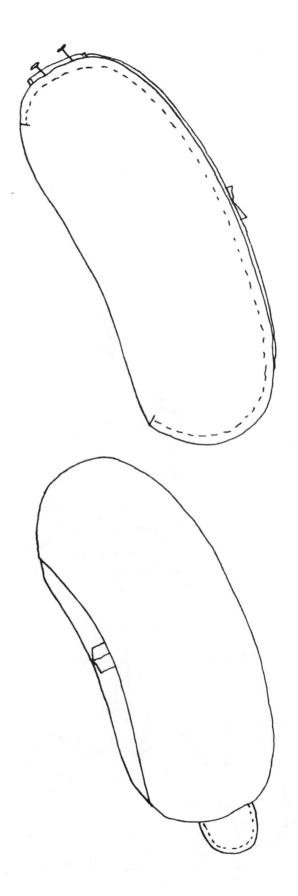

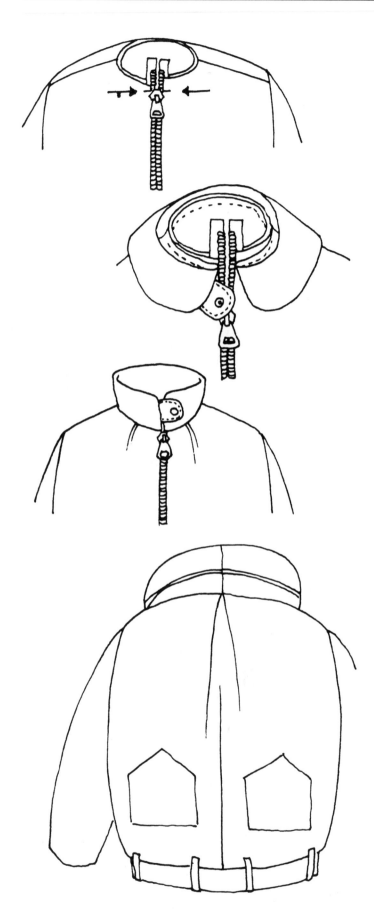

7. Pin the collar to the neck, right side of the collar to the right side of the jacket. Be sure to line up the neck edge of the collar ends with any mark you've made to establish your even neck heights.

8. Leave the lining of the collar free. Pin the lining of the jacket in with the body of the jacket though.

Make sure that you keep all the raw edges in line with one another, unless you have marked a matching centre point at the jacket front. If so, pin the collar at this point.

9. Line up the finished edge of the collar with the finished edge of the jacket front. This will enable you to stitch the zipper end right into the collar.

10. If the jacket neck is too big for the collar, simply put a box pleat at the centre back of the jacket, or a small pleat 2 to 3 cm (an inch or so) back from the front zipper on either side.

11. Whatever you do, make sure that both sides of the jacket match, and don't stitch the neck in until the jacket hangs right with its pleats. If you pleat the jacket, do the lining with it.

12. Sew the collar to the jacket.

13. Fold the edge of the collar lining under and sew it just at the sewing line you made sewing the collar on.

14. Topstitch the collar, about .5 cm (¼ inch) in from the edge, with a long stitch.

Finishing

1. You should have enough lining sticking out of the sleeves to roll under an edge in line with the hem of the jacket sleeve.

2. To finish the sleeve end, if you don't have a free arm on your sewing machine, you may have to slipstitch the lining to the jacket. You can slipstitch this down anyway, if you wish, but if the lining and sleeve are lined up perfectly at the stitch line, you should be able to machine stitch them together and have it look quite neat.

Don't go for coffee yet, you're almost done!

3. Open the jacket out and smooth the lining evenly down to the waistband of the jacket.

4. If there are no belt loops on the jacket, you can fold the lining under and sew it to the top of the waistband, overlapping it just enough for you to sew along the original sewing line of the waistband.

5. If the waistband has belt loops, finish the lining at the bottom edge of the waistband.

6. If the waistband is elasticized, stretch it as you sew the lining in.

So there you go. You're done! Now see if it fits.

4. Notes

Adult Pants Too Wide

If this is the case, you can put a pleat, or a small belt at the back sides of the waistband to snug the waist up, but if the pants are way too big you'll have to take the waistband right off to make it shorter or replace it with a ribbed waistband.

Adult Pants Too Short

1. If the adult pants are too short to get a jacket body and sleeves out of them, you have a couple of options. You can get the jacket body from one pair of pants and the sleeves from another, or you can take the sleeves from an old sweater or sweatshirt instead.

2. Another possibility is to lengthen the sleeves by sticking in an insert. If you can get a length of leather or heavy-duty cloth,

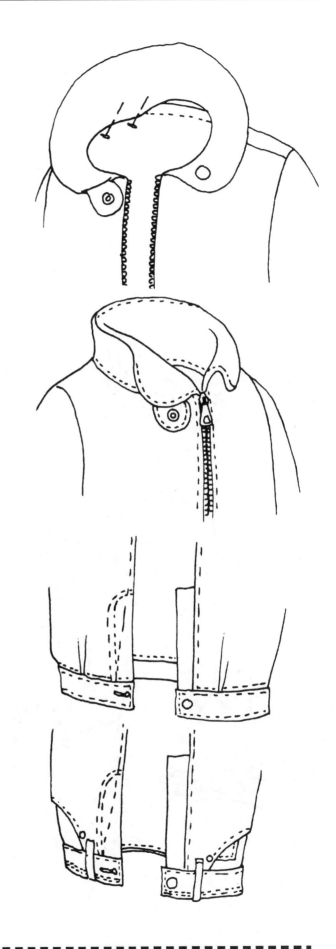

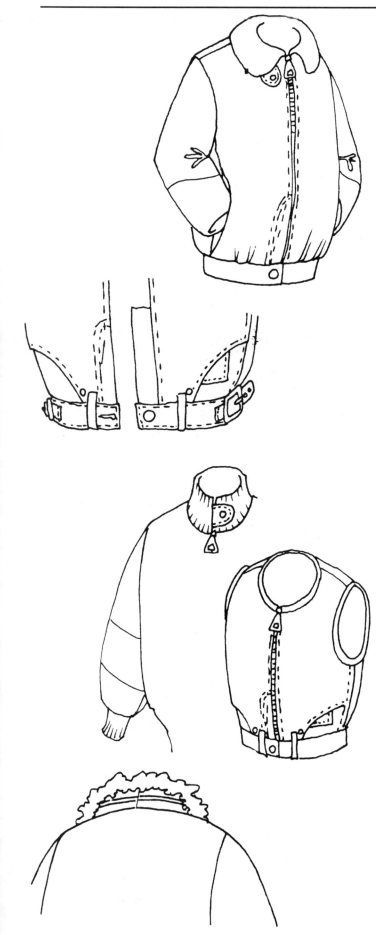

put it right at the elbow. If you can't get really tough cloth, put something soft just up from the cuff for warming cold noses. (See diagram.)

3. Still another possibility is to lengthen the jacket body by making a shoulder yoke out of any bright, tough material. To do this, cut out a yoke and pin, then sew it into place on the jacket front and back before you mark the jacket body. Be very careful, in this case, that the left sides are at the same height as the right sides.

Suggestions

1. Appliqué on the jacket back is fun, but it's best applied before you sew the shoulder seams.

2. If the waistband of the adult garment is too tight for your child's hips, but the pants have pleats, cut off all but the button or snap part of the waistband and replace it with elastic ribbing. Use the same ribbing to finish the cuffs and collar.

3. Keep an eye out for side vent pocket jeans with pleats. They make great jackets, because they have functional pockets and are perfect for the drop-waist bomber jacket style.

4. If you can get some pile (the lining from an old coat), it makes a great lining in a denim jacket. Just cut the pile lining a little narrower than the jacket itself, especially in the sleeves, or the jacket will be too bulky. The easiest way to do this is to cut the lining with no seam allowance anywhere except at the waistband and sleeve ends for hemming.

5. If you want to make a vest, simply leave off the sleeves and finish the armholes with seam binding or a strip of lining cut on the bias.

Remember to have fun!

CHAPTER THREE

Jeans to Jumpers

Designing and
making
children's
jumpers from
adult pants

1. Measure

1. Measure your child, (not always as easy as it sounds) according to the diagram.

2. Measure the inseam leg of the adult garment to be sure that it's long enough to accommodate the full dress length of the child.

3. If you're working with a straight or tapered leg in the adult pant, then you may find that the thigh is the widest part of the leg. In this case, turn the garment upside down and mark the jumper top at the cuff and the jumper hem at the top of the thigh.

4. If you're working with some really dated pants with a bell-bottom or an elephant-styled leg (remember them?) then the thigh may, in fact, be the narrowest part of the pant leg. If this is the case, the jumper top should be traced on the thigh while the hem is at the cuff of the original pant.

5. Whichever end is to be the jumper top, be sure to measure the circumference at this point. The sum of both legs must be several centimetres (a few inches) greater than the child's chest measurement. If it's too close a fit, the child will not be able to pull it on.

6. If the pants are too short or too narrow (there's no such thing as too wide), don't despair. Refer to NOTES for some helpful suggestions.

7. Measure out enough material for a facing or lining and prewash it to be sure that it will not shrink later. Remember that you're working with used jeans or cords for the jumper, so the fabric is completely pre-shrunk. If the lining has not been shrunk yet, the finished garment will pucker up quite badly after the first wash.

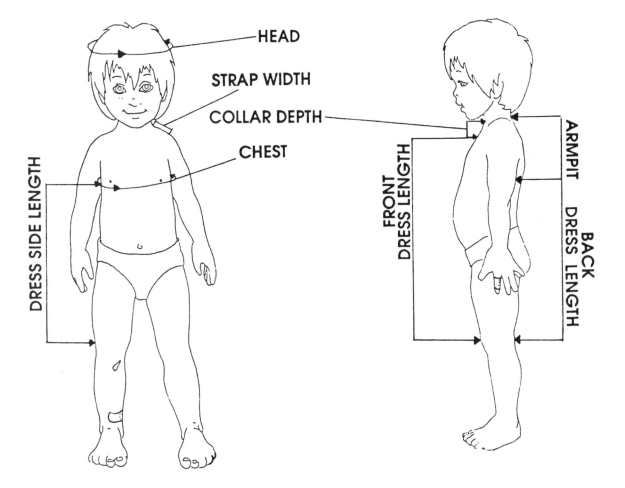

2. Mark

If the jeans you are working with have a particularly fancy side seam, you may want to use this as the centre seam of the jumper front and back. Otherwise, merely establish which seam is to be the centre and use the same seam from both pant legs.

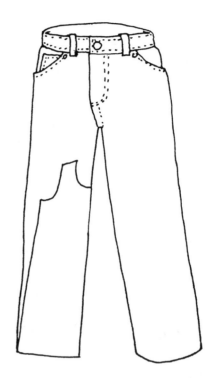

✂ IF YOU'VE MADE A PATTERN *(see page 119)*

1. Smooth the pants out flat so that the legs are evenly folded from the desired centre seam.

2. Place the jumper front pattern with the centre line along the centre seam of the pant leg. Be careful to line up the hem of the jumper with the hem of the pant leg. If you are using the pant leg upside down, place the shoulder point of the pattern at the base of the pant hem. This is to ensure that both halves of the finished jumper are the same width. Trace the pattern with dressmaker's chalk or any washable pencil.

3. Repeat for the pattern back on the other pant leg, being careful, as mentioned above, to place the pattern piece in the same place on the adult pant leg as you did the jumper front pattern.

4. Cut out the front and back jumper pieces, *double thickness*.

5. For facing instructions skip to step 14 of If You Haven't Made a Pattern.

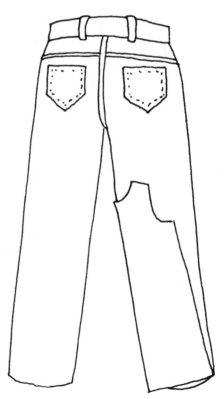

✂ IF YOU HAVEN'T MADE A PATTERN

Select guides **E** and **G**.

1. Whichever seam you choose for the centre of the garment, measure up it to your desired centre front height on one leg and your desired centre back height on the other.

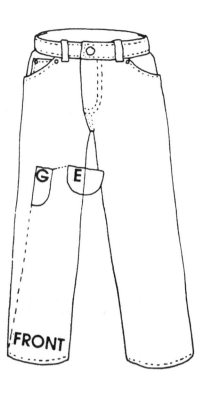

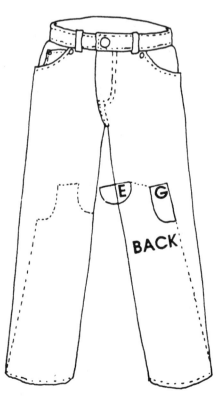

2. Place your front neck guide **E** at this point on the first leg and the back neck guide **E** at this point on the other leg.

3. Trace the guides.

4. Measure across, and slightly down, from the high point of each neck curve and mark your desired shoulder width. Make sure that you use the same measurement and the same slight angle for both shoulders.

5. Place the armpit guide **G** at the outside point of the shoulder line, and trace the curve.

6. Repeat for the other shoulder.

7. Measure straight across the jumper from the bottom of the armpit guide to the centre seam for both front and back.

8. Add these two measurements and multiply by two. This number must be at least 10 cm (4 inches) greater than the child's chest measurement. If it's not, and you still have room in the pant leg, angle the armpit guide out a bit or widen the shoulders (you may need to do both) to achieve the needed chest size.

9. If the curve of the armpit guide still seems to be too far from the side seam of the pant leg, drop a line from the bottom end of the armpit guide to the corner of the closest seam and the hem.

10. Repeat for the other leg. You should now have the front and back halves of your jumper traced on the adult jeans.

11. If the armpit curve comes almost to the seam of the pant leg, simply extend the curve right out to the seam and pick it open or cut it off.

12. Once your jumper is marked to your satisfaction (and looks as much like the illustrations as possible, maybe even better), smooth the pant legs out from your chosen centre seams.

13. Place your scissors in the hand of your choice, take a deep breath and cut out your jumper, *double thickness,* on the lines you have marked.

All going well, you should now have the front and back half of your jumper.

This is probably a good time to take a break. On the other hand, if your child or children are still busy, sleeping or in someone else's care, you may prefer to keep going. You're almost done!

14. Lay out your lining or facing fabric and place the jumper halves on it, right sides together. If you're only doing a facing, be sure to lay the jumper out so that all the side seams of the facing are as close as possible to the same length.

15. Trace the jumper pieces onto the lining or facing material and cut out what you've traced.

16. If you're lining the jumper and using the original hem of the jeans, be sure to cut the lining longer than the cut-out jumper. Otherwise you will not have enough lining to fold under for a hem to match the jumper.

3. *Make*

Plain Jumper

1. Sew the side seams of the jumper, right sides together.

2. Sew the side seams of the lining or facing, right sides together.

3. Sew the shoulder seams of the jumper, right sides together. Check to be sure that you're sewing the left shoulders together and the right shoulders together. It's very easy to sew the two front shoulders together and the two back shoulders together by mistake. When this happens, you end up

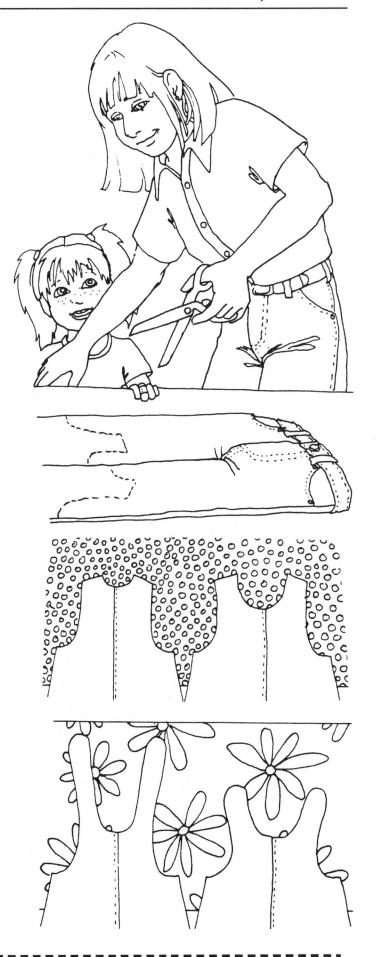

with one very large armhole and one very small one. The neckline also tends to be large and the shoulders don't sit right.

4. Repeat step 3 for the shoulders of the facing.

5. Turn the jumper inside out and place the facing inside the top. Line up the side seams and make sure that you have the facing front lined up with the jumper front. Be sure the right sides are together.

6. Sew the neckline, then turn the jumper right side out and turn the facing to the inside of the jumper.

7. Fold under an edge on the armholes and the armhole facing or lining and pin the two together, being careful to line up the underarm and shoulder seams.

8. If you're a perfectionist, you can slipstitch the armholes together and then topstitch. If you're in a hurry, topstitch the armholes together.

9. Tack the facing down. If you're lining the jumper, smooth the lining out carefully and fold under the bottom edge to match the hem on the jumper. For a little extra colour you could even allow the lining to extend below the hem enough to fold over as a bit of bright trim.

Now stitch the two together.

10. If you're not using the original pant hem for your finished garment, you may now hem the jumper.

If you are, congratulations, you're done.

Fastenable Shoulder Strap Style

Refer to step 16 of the section on jumpers in Chapter 10, Guides and Patternmaking. There are instructions there for variations to jumper tops.

1. Proceed as you would for a plain jumper but skip steps 3 and 4.

2. When you come to sew the facing or lining to the jumper, you don't just sew the neck. Because the neck and armholes are finished with straps, you can sew the entire top of the facing or lining to the jumper in one continuous line of sewing.

If necessary, clip your curves. This will help the neck and armholes to lie smoothly. It's particularly important if you work with a generous seam allowance or if you have some tight curves.

3. Turn the jumper right side out and turn the facing or lining to the inside.

4. Topstitch with a long stitch about .25 cm (1/8 inch) in from the folded edge on the right side.

5. Return to step 9 of the plain jumper at this point and continue on through to the end.

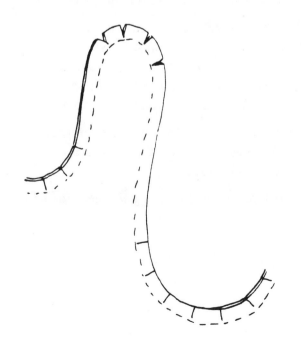

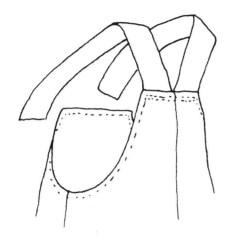

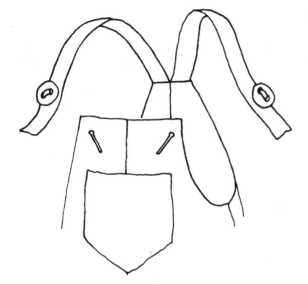

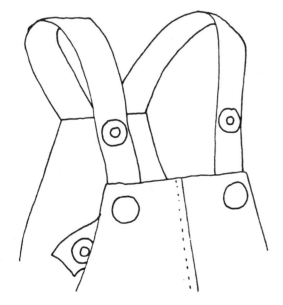

Bib-top Jumper

Once again, for variations to the style of the jumper top refer to step 16 of the section on jumpers in Chapter 10, Guides and Patternmaking.

1. You construct a bib-top jumper in almost exactly the same fashion as you would a fastenable strap jumper. Before you go to step 2, though, you need to cut two matching lengths of elastic.

2. Measure your child according to the diagram in chapter one for a shoulder strap and add about 10 cm (4 inches). This should be a good length for the elastic.

3. Cut one end of the elastic square and the other at about a 45-degree angle.

4. Place the angled ends of the elastics between the facing or lining and the jumper at the back bib. Line the points of the angles up at the back centre seam. Pin them in place.

5. Now proceed to step 2 of the fastenable shoulder strap jumper above. When you sew the back of the lining or facing to the jumper, it's a good idea to run a double line of stitching to secure the elastic straps. Do the same with the topstitching at the back.

6. Make buttonholes in the bib or apply the bib half of snaps. You should wait to apply the buttons or the other half of the snaps until after you've established the right location with the child in the jumper.

7. To finish, return to step 9 of the plain jumper style above, and continue right through to the end.

Now all you need to do is get your child to try it on.

4. Notes

Adult Pants Too Short

If the jeans you are hoping to use turn out to be too short, don't give up. You have a variety of options open to you.

1. The easiest is to try a larger pair of jeans, (unless, of course, you have your heart set on this particular pair).

2. Make the bib-top jumper, as it requires less length than the other two styles.

3. Make the skirt for the jumper from one pair of jeans and the yoke top from another pair or from a remnant of upholstery fabric. Any fairly heavy remnant from your scrap box would do fine.

To do this, you merely use the guides to make the yoke out of whatever fabric you've chosen. Trace the yoke on your lining fabric for a yoke lining.

Sew the yoke and lining as you would for a regular jumper.

For the skirt, simply measure the length of skirt you want to attach to the yoke and cut off both pant legs at this length. Open the easiest seam in the pant legs and sew the two legs together to form one large tube of sorts.

Gather the top edge of the skirt tube to fit the bottom of the yoke and sew them together, right sides facing.

Smooth the yoke lining down, fold the edge under and pin it to cover the gathered edge of the skirt. Slipstitch, or machine stitch, to finish, and hem in the usual fashion.

There is a great deal of room for creativity in this particular style of jumper. When you attach the skirt to the yoke you can sew in an apron at the same time, or piping, or lace, or whatever your imagination can cook up.

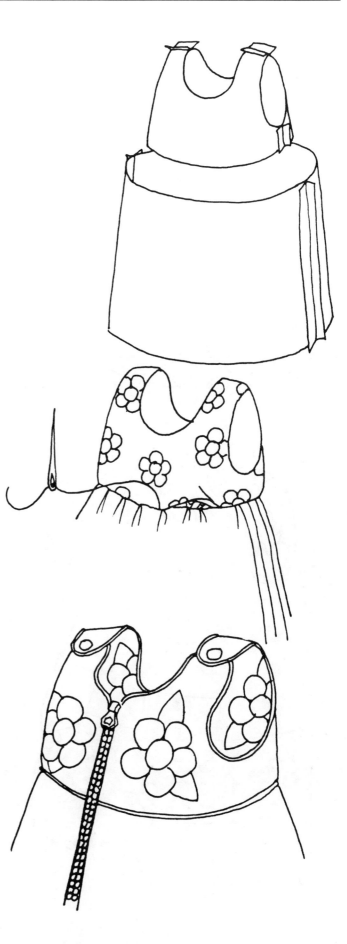

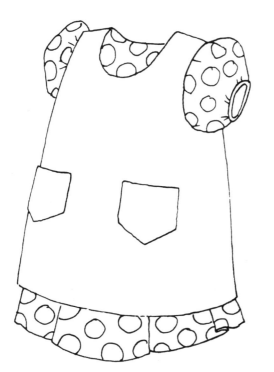

For an even fuller skirt in this style, open the front skirt seam and insert a wide band of the same fabric you are using for the facing. Try a bit of the same fabric for pocket linings and appliqué on the yoke front.

4. If the jeans of your choice are only 5 to 10 cm (2 to 4 inches) too short, you might consider putting in a full lining that extends below the hem of the jumper itself to serve as an attractive underskirt.

In this case, cut the lining 8 to 10 cm (3 or 4 inches) longer than you want it. In order to have the lining facing right side in for the top of the jumper and right side out (to show under the skirt) at the bottom, cut the skirt off the lining at about chest level.

Now reverse the skirt of the lining and re-apply to the top, right side to wrong side. This way, when you attach the lining to the jumper, the right side shows below the hem, but you also have the right side showing for the top of the lining.

If you have any lining material left over in this case, you might try making little puff sleeves and turning the jumper into a dress. To do this, simply trace the armhole guide, end to end, and extend a line the desired sleeve length out from the point of the curve at both ends.

Angle these lines out for a full sleeve or keep them straight for a narrow sleeve.

Sew the underarm seam and insert the sleeve into the finished jumper before you attach the lining or facing. Then you can contain the raw sleeve edge in the folded edge of the lining or facing.

5. Another quick way to lengthen the jumper is to carefully draw a line 5 to 10 cm (2 to 4 inches) up from the hem and cut the hem off. Sew in a band of brocade or some tough fabric of your choice. Try to choose a fabric the same weight as the jumper itself. Be sure the band is cut evenly and wide enough to give the jumper the desired length when you reattach the hem you cut off.

6. You can buy wide, pregathered eyelet lace and sew it right under the jumper hem to add extra length, or you can create your own ruffle with scraps of lining.

If the skirt is really short, create layers of ruffle using denim and lining material alternately.

Adult Pants Too Narrow

1. If the jeans you have selected are wide enough to fit your child with a bit of breathing room, but too narrow for a pull-on, then find a good, bright zipper, at least 30 to 35 cm (12 to 14 inches) long and insert it in the front or the back seam. This may mean you are going to have a fairly straight-cut jumper. In this case, you might want to cut the jumper shorter so the child can move around.

If you'd rather keep it long, open up the entire jumper front, put in a long, open-ended zipper, and finish the edges below the zipper.

2. If the jeans you've selected are impossibly narrow, don't worry. You can fix that too.

The easiest solution is to mark the jeans from the centre and open up the side seams. You will find, in this case, that you are short of material in the underarm.

Cut two strips of matching denim, or similar weight material, longer than the side seam of the jumper. You can cut straight strips, or flared strips for a fuller skirt. Sew these strips to the jumper's front side seams, lining up the hem end and having your extra hang off at the top end.

Lay your guide along the armpit curve again and draw the missing piece of underarm. Flip the guide and draw the other half of the missing underarm. Then cut the desired curve along the line you've

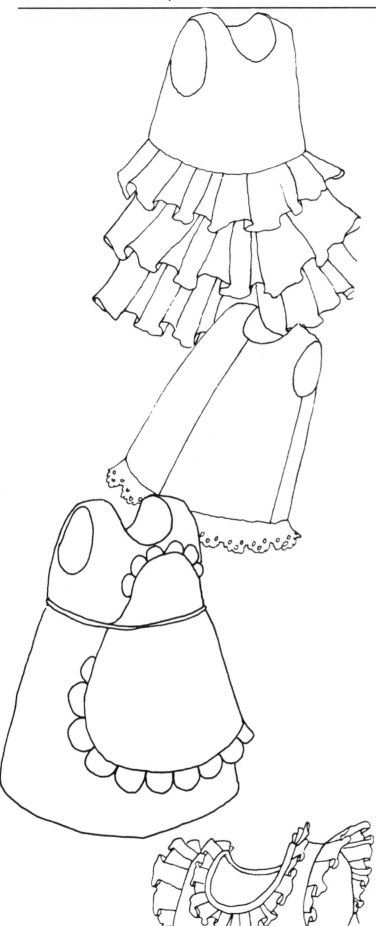

marked. Sew the strip to the side seam of the back half of the jumper. Finish the jumper in the usual fashion.

3. A faster variation on this solution is to simply open the front and back centre seams and place your inserts there. In this case, you lay your armpit guides down first and work towards the centre of the jumper.

If you have used side panels to widen the jumper, especially bright side panels, you can achieve a very attractive finish by attaching the original pants pockets across these panels.

Adult Pants Too Wide

There's no such animal. If the jeans you have selected are enormously wide, rejoice. You have the opportunity to make a gathered, yoke-topped jumper or a jumper that is gathered or pleated at the front and back neck.

You could also make a flared skirt on the jumper. Simply place the guides so that the area to be gathered is the guide curve that is extended, then gather the extended part to match the original guide.

You may find it easier to finish a gathered or pleated neck with bias tape. This you can buy or create by cutting a 4-cm (1½-inch) strip from lining scraps. Satin ribbon works fine too. Satin ribbon works fine too. Just be sure it's cloth ribbon, not paper or plastic.

If you really have your heart set on an A-line jumper, then only use as much of the jeans as you want and save the rest for when you are working with a pair of pants that are a little small.

Just remember to take it one step at a time, and have fun.

Shirts to Coats and Dresses

Designing and making children's coats and dresses from adult shirts

1. Measure

1. Measure the child for whom you will be sewing, or one who is about the same size. Refer to the diagram for directions.

2. Measure the adult shirt, to be sure that it's long enough to fit the child as a dress.

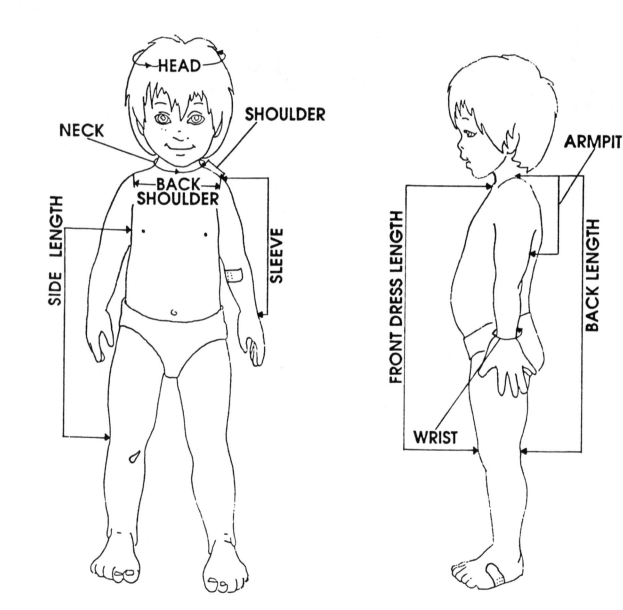

2. Mark

✂ **IF YOU'VE MADE A PATTERN** (*see page 119*)

1. Place the sleeve pattern on the sleeve of the shirt, lining up the long edge of the pattern with the long folded edge of the sleeve. If you wish to use the cuff of the adult shirt, line up the cuff end of the pattern with the cuff edge of the shirt.

2. For a fuller sleeve, move the pattern up to the shoulder end of the adult sleeve and either cut off the original cuff and reapply it or gather the sleeve end.

3. Place the dress front pattern on the shirt front, being careful to line up the centre of the pattern with the shirt centre. If you wish to use the original collar and shoulders of the adult garment, simply place the shoulders of the pattern on the shoulders of the shirt and mark the armpits and the hem only.

If you wish to creat a new neck and shoulder line, move the pattern down to a point about 4 cm (1½ inches) above a button. This will allow you to make a finished neckline that already has a button and buttonhole. If you're really in a hurry, move the pattern down far enough to use the original hem of the shirt for the dress or coat you're designing.

4. Flip the shirt and do the same using the dress back pattern.

5. Cut the shirt as marked.

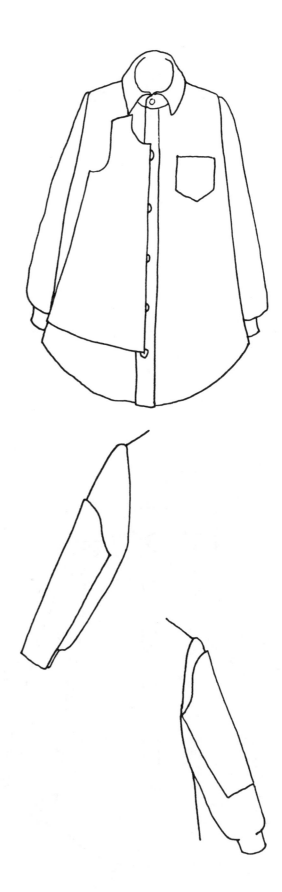

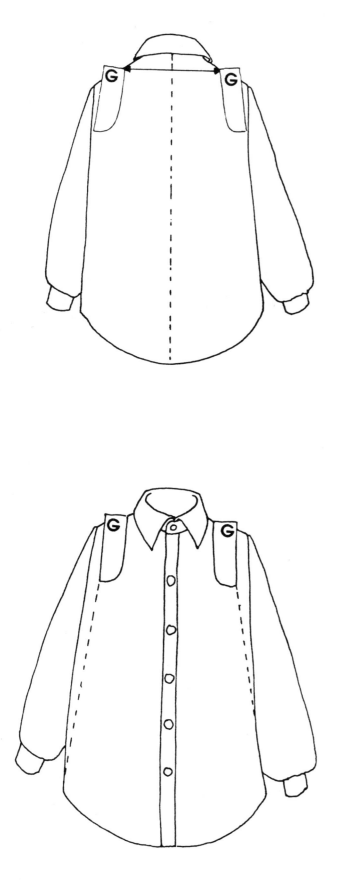

✂ **IF YOU HAVEN'T MADE A PATTERN**

Select guides **E**, **F** and **G**.

Using the Adult Collar

1. If you wish to use the original collar and cuffs from the adult shirt, you won't need the neck guides this time. Keep in mind though, that the neck on an adult shirt is bound to be more than a little loose on a child. If this is what you want, great. You're almost finished.

2. Take the child's shoulder back measurement and divide it in half.

3. Measure this amount, plus 1.5 cm (½ inch) for seam allowance, out from the centre of the shirt in both directions.

4. Place the armpit guide **G** at this point on each side of the shirt front. You may have to play with the angle of the armpit guide here to keep it from lying on top of the sleeves. In any case, do your best to make sure the left side matches the right when you are finished.

5. Draw a line from the bottom of the armpit guide out to the side of the shirt at the desired side length.

6. Repeat for the shirt back, matching the front armpit curve ends.

7. Mark your desired centre front length on the shirt. Do the same for your desired centre back length.

8. Connect the side hem points and the centre hem points with a gently curving line. Trace the hem from another dress or jumper if you have difficulty here.

9. Smooth the sleeves out from the underarm seam and measure the child's sleeve length up from the cuff toward the shoulder. Place the sleeve guide **F** at this point. Try to make the angle of the guide match the angle of the original shirt armhole.

10. Trace the guide and then flip it to repeat for the other sleeve.

11. Now hack away! Or, in more professional words, cut the shirt as marked.

It's often easiest to get the sleeves to match by cutting one first and then using it as a pattern for the second sleeve. Just be sure that you have the sleeves lined up properly. To do this, place the sleeve openings together and then line up underarm seams and cuffs. Otherwise it's very easy to get two left or two right sleeves.

This may be a good time to check your watch and make sure you haven't got a forlorn child waiting for you on the school steps somewhere. If all are present or accounted for in some way, take a break. You've earned it.

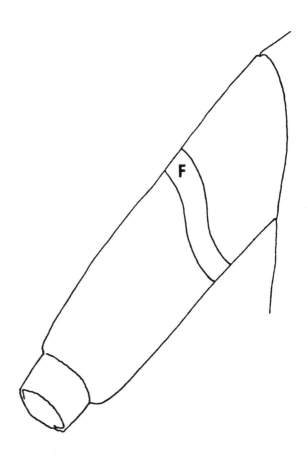

Creating a New Neckline

1. If you are not using the existing collar of the adult shirt, then you may be able to use the hem.

2. Measure your child's front dress length up the shirt front from the hem. Place the front neck guide **E** at this point, matching the centre line with that of the shirt.

3. Trace the curve.

4. Extend a line on a down-sloping angle from each side of the neck. Measure your child's shoulder width along this line and mark it clearly.

Do this for both sides, but be sure they are as close to identical as possible.

5. Place the flat end of the armpit guide **G** at the end of each shoulder line. Make sure that the points of the armpit guide come out the same amount on each side from the centre line of the dress. This distance should be a quarter of your desired dress chest measurement.

■■

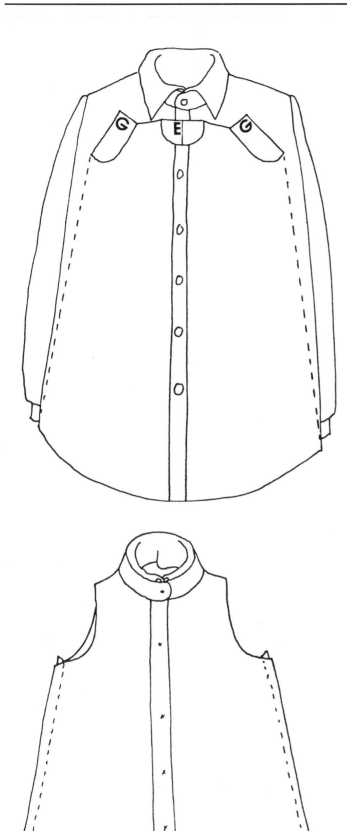

If you have a large shirt and you want a fairly full dress, bring the point of the armpit guide right out to the sides of the shirt. It's very important to remember, though, that whatever you do to one side of the shirt you have to do to the other to make the sides match. (This doesn't include things like pockets and appliqué.)

6. If the armpit guide angles out too severely, you may want to make the shoulders wider instead and gather or pleat them to fit the child. Once again, be sure the two shoulders match.

7. Flip the shirt and repeat the process, this time using the back neck guide.

Check that the back shoulders match the front shoulders.

8. Go back to step 9 of Using the Adult Collar and carry on from there.

3. Make

1. One last time, check to be sure that the garment you have cut out will fit the child you measured a while ago. Otherwise you may find that you've started your Christmas sewing earlier than you planned. (That's if you're lucky enough to have a friend or relative who'll fit the garment.)

2. If you're using the existing collar of the shirt, sew the side seams and insert the sleeves. Be careful to keep the cuff opening to the back.

3. Sew your hem and you're done. Really! That's it!

4. If you're using the original hem of the shirt and the original side seam, sew your shoulder seams, gathering where necessary, and insert the sleeves.

5. Use a strip of bias tape or a length of lace to finish the neckline. If you were not able to place your neckline directly above an existing button, you may need to add a buttonhole and button.

6. Locate your child and see if the garment fits.

4. Notes

Making a dress from an adult shirt is a very easy process. It can also be done without the addition of any notions, so it's a very inexpensive and fast Short Kutz. This leaves you a great deal of room to play with any bits around the house and your imagination. It also makes this Short Kutz a particularly good one to make with your child, if you're so inclined.

Collars

1. If you have an old party dress with a perfect little lace collar that has escaped whatever disaster befell the dress, pick it off and apply it to the dress you're making.

2. The ribbing from an old sweater is a good coat collar.

3. Some pregathered eyelet lace and bright bias tape can be very pretty, especially if you make your own bias tape with scraps from the shirt.

4. If you really know how to sew and are feeling terribly ambitious, pick off the original adult collar, dismantle it, cut it down to size and reapply it.

5. If you have enough fabric left from the shirt, cut a strip 8 to 10 cm (3 or 4 inches) wide and twice the length of the child's neck measurement. Fold this strip in half along its length, right sides together and finish the end. Then turn it right side out and

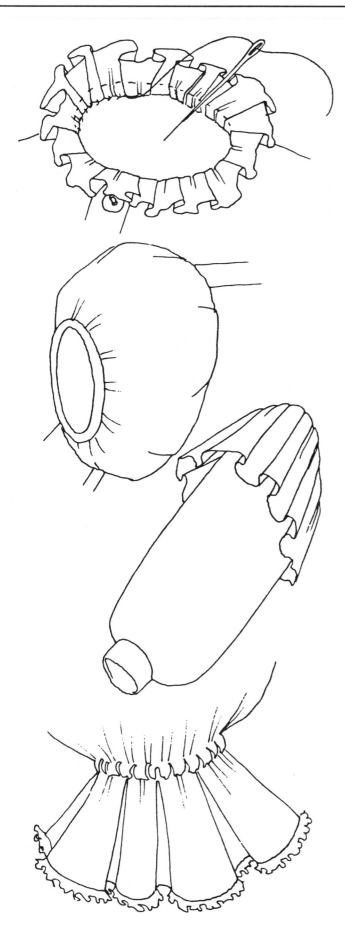

gather it to fit the neck. Sew it to the right side of the neck, then fold under and topstitch the raw edge down inside the neck line.

Sleeves

1. If you've gone with a lace collar, use the top end of the adult sleeve so that you can have a puffy sleeve, and put lace and elastic at the cuff. This whole effect can be tied together with more of the same lace peeking out from beneath the hem.

2. If the adult sleeves are torn or stained at the elbows, try short puffy sleeves.

3. Another option with damaged elbows is a two-tone sleeve. Simply cut out the worn section of the original sleeve and replace it with a band of matching or contrasting fabric. Just be sure to make sure the inserts are the same width and in the same place on the sleeve.

4. A double sleeve also solves the problem of damaged elbows, and it's easier than it sounds.

Cut your short oversleeve from the shirt sleeve and use it as a pattern for the undersleeve.

Cut the long undersleeve from any fabric (even an old sheet) that complements the shirt material. Make sure that the shoulder end matches the oversleeve, but be sure to cut the undersleeve long enough to fit your child. You may want to apply the original shirt cuff at the end of the undersleeve.

Hem the oversleeve and finish it with lace if you'd like. Place the undersleeve inside the oversleeve and insert the two into the dress armhole together.

5. Bright piping around the armhole is a pretty accent, especially if it matches the buttons on the shirt or a ruffle on the skirt.

6. You may want to save the sleeve from this shirt for another project and put in white sleeves with a matching collar on this dress.

Hems

1. If your dress looks like it's going to be too short, use a wide band of eyelet lace, gathered, sewn right under the hem. This gives the look of a petticoat and adds some length to the dress.

2. You may find that you have a length of plain fabric that complements the shirt. In this case you could use it for a ruffle at the hem.

3. You might want to use the shirt to make an overdress to extend the life of a pretty white summer dress.

In this case you leave the sleeves off the shirt dress and finish the neck and armholes with seam binding. Make it a little shorter than the underdress too.

You actually end up with several combinations this way. You have the white summer dress; the shirt dress is a sun dress by itself; together they make a spring and fall dress; and if you use the shirt dress with a sweater and tights it works great for the winter too.

Bits and Pieces

Whatever style of garment you choose, take advantage of all the detailing and finishing on the original garment. Use the pockets, pearl snaps, piping on yokes, or labels, and then add your own imagination. Try appliqués, bright buttons, lace, ribbons, bells, old brooches—whatever your scrap box and budget will allow.

Please keep in mind that you're supposed to be having a little fun too.

CHAPTER FIVE

Shirts to Tops and Pants

Designing and
making
children's
tops and
pants from
adult shirts

1. Measure

1. Measure your child according to the diagram. Resist the urge to administer a tranquilizer first.

2. Measure the sleeve of the adult shirt. Be sure that it's long enough to accommodate the outside seam length of the child's pants plus at least 4 cm (1 1/2 inches) for a waistband.

3. Check the sleeve width at the armpit to be sure that it's wide enough to accommodate your child's hips plus several centimetres (a few inches). This is to allow for seam allowance and room to move. To do this, measure the sleeve width (as opposed to the circumference) and subtract 6 or 7 cm (2½ inches). Now multiply by four.

If the resulting figure is smaller than or just a little larger than your child's hips, the sleeves are too narrow to make pants for your child.

Don't lose heart though. If you can't find a larger shirt or you are simply nuts about using this particular one, refer to some of the suggestions in NOTES (or find a smaller child).

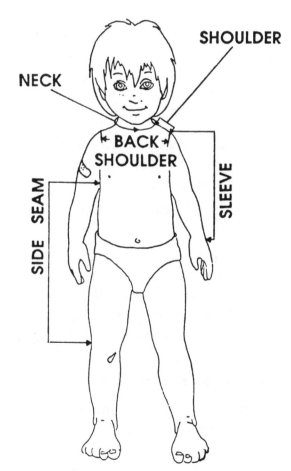

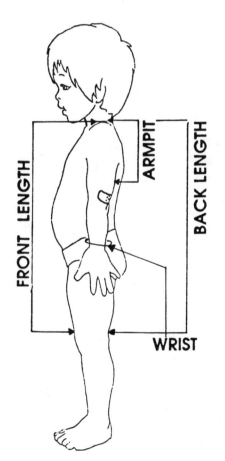

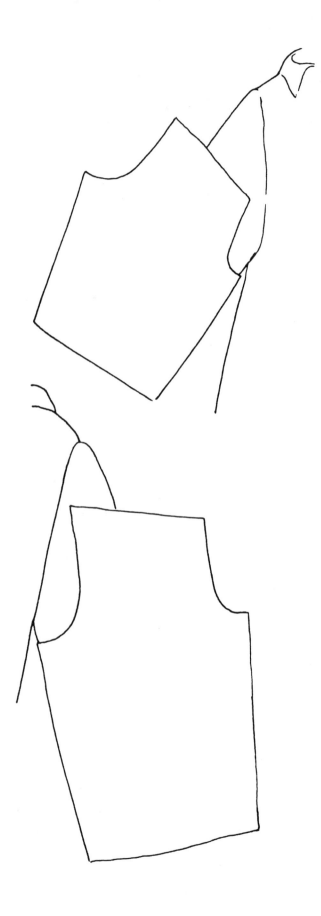

2. Mark

✂ **IF YOU'VE MADE PATTERNS** *(see page 115, 116)*

Pants

1. Smooth the shirt out face up. This will ensure that the bottom side of the cuffs will be face down.

2. Place the pants pattern on the sleeve so that the front crotch inseam is lined up with the underarm seam of the shirt sleeve. Be careful to have the cuff end of the pattern even with the edge of the shirt cuff. If the centre lies well outside the edge of the shirt sleeve, the sleeve is too narrow for pants.

If the pattern centre line lies well within the shirt sleeve edge, you may have the option of a baggy pair of trousers. If this is the case, design some extra length into the pants as well for extended wear and greater comfort. Trace the pattern with dressmaker's chalk or any washable pencil.

3. Repeat for the other sleeve, being sure that the inseam length matches the one on the first sleeve.

4. Turn the shirt over and smooth it out, face down.

5. This time, place the back inseam line of the pants pattern against the underarm seam of the shirt sleeve. Make sure the inseam of the back pattern half lines up with the one you marked on the front. Trace the pattern.

6. Repeat for the other sleeve.

7. Cut out the pants as marked, remembering to cut *single thickness*.

Tunic or Top

1. Smooth the shirt out again, face up, and place the tunic or top pattern front on the shirt front. Be sure the centre line is on the centre front of the shirt. If you're using the original collar, place the shoulders of the pattern on the shoulders of the shirt.

If you're creating a new collar, place the pattern 4 cm (1½ inches) above a button. This will make it easier to finish the collar later. Trace the pattern.

2. Flip the shirt and place the back pattern piece for a tunic or top on the back of the shirt, carefully lining up the centre line of the pattern with the centre of the shirt back. Once again, if you're using the original collar, place the pattern shoulders on the shirt shoulders.

If you're creating a new neckline, line up the bottom of the armpit curves from the back pattern piece with those you've already marked on the shirt front.

3. Cut the shirt out as marked, remembering to cut *single thickness.*

✂ IF YOU HAVEN'T MADE PATTERNS

Select guides **A, B, E, F** and **G**.

Pants

1. With the shirt right side up, measure up the underarm seam of the sleeve from the cuff the desired inseam length. You may want to add about 5 cm (2 inches) for growth and activity. Mark this point clearly.

2. Place the front crotch guide **B** at this point and trace the curve.

Add 5 cm (2 inches) to this line to allow for the waistband.

3. Repeat for the other sleeve.

4. Cut a length of 2-cm (¾-inch) elastic 1.5 cm (½ inch) or so shorter than the child's waist measurement.

5. Flip the shirt to lie face down and repeat the above steps on the sleeve backs, this time using the back crotch guide **A**. Be sure

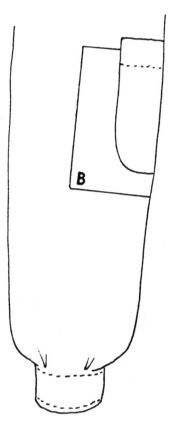

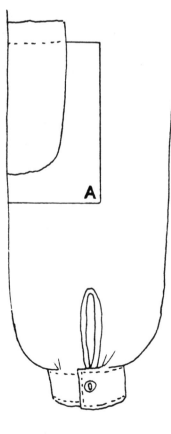

to match your inseam points with those marked on the front of the sleeves.

6. Draw a line with dressmaker's chalk on each sleeve, connecting the front crotch line with the back crotch line. There is likely to be a slight angle to this line, rising towards the back. This is normal as the seat of any pair of pants tends to rise higher than the front. This is also necessary to accommodate the child's rear end and allow room for movement.

If you wish to allow extra room for movement, you might even want to raise the back waistband a little bit higher than your measurements would indicate. This is particularly true if your child is still in diapers.

7. Cut out each sleeve *single thickness* as you have marked it.

Tunic or Top

1. Keep the shirt face down. If you're using the original collar, measure out, from the back centre point of the neck, half the desired shoulder back width in each direction. (If you don't plan to use the original collar, skip to step 9.)

2. Place the top point of the armpit guide G at this point on either side.

3. Trace the curves.

4. From the bottom point of the armpit curves, measure out the desired side length. Angle this line out until it touches the side seam of the shirt. Clearly mark this point.

5. Flip the shirt and measure the desired front length down the front of the shirt from the neck.

6. Flip the shirt again and measure the desired back length down the centre back from the neck.

7. Connect the marked side lengths with the front and back centre marks. This can be done with a straight line, but with a fuller hem it's a good idea to draw a gentle curve instead. If you don't feel up to eyeballing a gentle curve, trace the curve from the hem of another dress or jumper.

8. Cut the side seams and armpits *double thickness*.

9. If you're not planning to use the collar of the original shirt, see if you can use the original hem instead. Remember that one of the ideas behind *Short Kutz* is to save time by using as many of the finished details on the adult garment as possible.

10. In this case, measure up the side seam your desired side length.

11. Place your armpit guide **G** here.

12. Measure up the shirt centre front your desired front length.

13. Place your front neck guide **E** at the top of this line. Be sure to centre the guide with the centre line.

14. Trace your guides and connect the top points to form the shoulders.

15. If the shoulder lines slope down towards the neck, move the neck guide up until they slope down towards the arm.

16. If you want to use the shirt tails themselves as a hem, measure up the front your desired front length, but skip the side seam measurement as you won't need it. Place the front neck guide **E**, lining up the centre line of the guide with the centre of the shirt, and trace it.

17. Measure and draw out your desired shoulder width, being careful to slope them down slightly to the arms. Be very careful, also, that both shoulders match. Place the flat end of the armpit guide **G** at each of the outer shoulder points. Make sure the armpit guide is angled out the same amount for each side of the shirt, either right to the side seams of the shirt, or in from the edge.

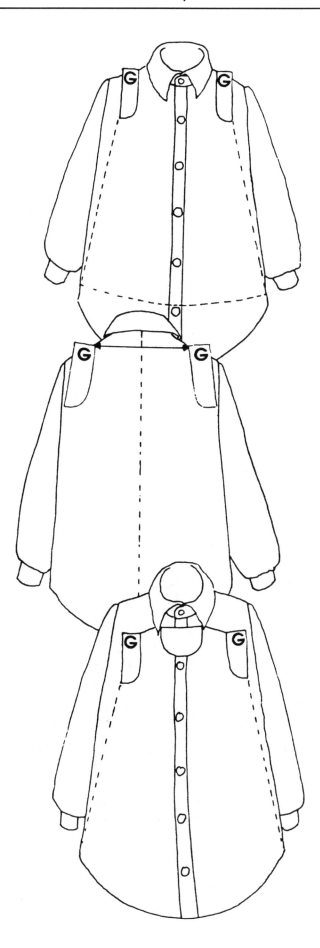

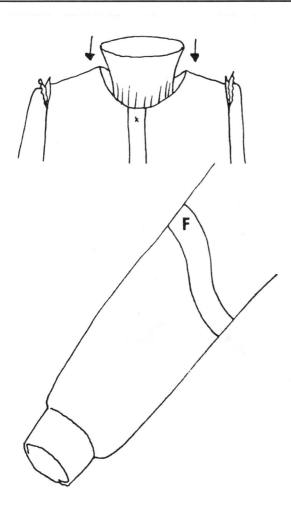

18. Flip the shirt and repeat the procedure on the back, using the back neck guide. Check to be sure that all your shoulder, neck and armpit points line up.

19. Cut the garment out of the shirt, *single thickness this time,* first the front and then the back.

20. The sleeves from this shirt have already been cut to make trousers, but if you want sleeves for the top, you have several options.

Cut the sleeves and neck from an old turtleneck and use them to finish the top. In this case, be sure the neck will fit as a pullover and simply sew the turtle neck into the neck hole.

Use the sleeves from another shirt that complements the colours in the shirt you've used for the tunic and pants.

Make sleeves using the pattern instructions for sleeve guide **F** and any remnant that matches the shirt.

You could also finish the armhole and the hem with a ruffle.

3. Make

Pants

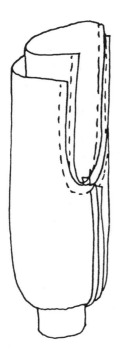

1. Take the shirt sleeves that you cut for trousers and turn one of them inside out.

2. Slip the right-side-out sleeve inside the inside-out sleeve.

3. Make sure the inseams are lined up and the cuffs pointed in the same direction and sew the two sleeves together along the crotch line.

4. Serge the waist or make a small fold along the edge before folding under the waist to form a casing for the elastic.

5. Sew the casing almost completely, but leave an opening for threading the elastic.

6. Thread the elastic (a safety pin helps) and sew it closed.

7. Close the casing.

Smile. The pants are done.

Tunic or Top

1. If you are using the collar in the adult shirt, sew your side seams.

2. Finish the armholes by rolling the edges or applying bias tape. You can make your own bias tape with any scrap of fabric that goes well with the shirt.

3. You can also use the armpit guides to make sleeves from new material (or be really cost efficient and make sleeves out of an old dress, old curtains or old sheets).

Just place the short, squared end of armpit guide **G** at the folded edge of your new fabric and trace the curve. Measure along the fold from the flat end of the armpit guide (this being the shoulder end) your desired sleeve length.

Draw a line the length of the child's wrist measurement, out at right angles from the fold at this point. Connect this line to the shoulder curve, and cut it out. Use this first sleeve, placed on the fold, to trace the second sleeve.

4. If you're working with stretch cotton, you can cut two rectangles of fabric that are as wide as the wrist measurement but twice as long as the depth you want the cuffs to be.

Cut another rectangle that will stretch enough to fit around the child's head but is twice as long as you want the neck to be.

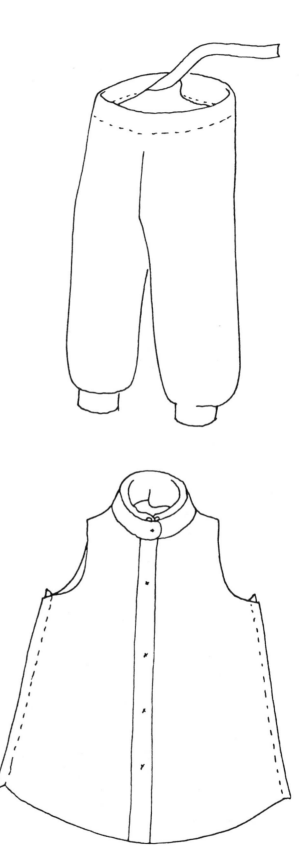

Sew each rectangle into a long tube, right sides together, and then turn them half right side out. You now have two cuffs and a turtleneck collar.

5. Turn the sleeves inside out. Insert the folded-over cuffs into the sleeves so that all three raw edges are together. Stretch the cuffs to fit the sleeves as you sew them together.

6. Do the same for the collar as you did for the sleeve cuffs. Keep the neck seam to the back.

7. To put sleeves in the top, turn it inside out and insert the sleeves, right side out. Make sure you line up the underarm seams before you sew them.

8. Sew the hem of your top and you're done.

9. If you're using the shirt hem for your dress and creating a new neckline, you've got room for lots of creativity.

10. If you have to gather the shoulders or the neck, do so before sewing the shoulder seams. If you're working with heavy material, you may be better off using pleats instead of gathers.

11. Sew the shoulders together.

12. Finish the collar with bias tape or a ready-made collar.

13. Collars can also be liberated from old shirts, dresses and sweaters.

Whatever your choice of finish, you're done. Really.

Now, where are the kids?

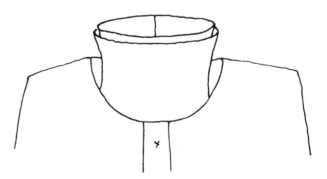

4. Notes

Adult Sleeves Too Narrow

If the sleeves of the original shirt are too narrow to make trousers, you can make a butterfly-shaped gusset or insert that extends from the front waist to the back waist.

1. To do this you first cut out the marked sleeves and measure the full length of the crotch seam.

2. Next, measure and cut a rectangular strip of fabric from shirt scraps or a similar, matching material. Make sure this strip is the same length as the crotch seam, but wide enough to make the pants fit. Don't forget to include at least a 1.5-cm (½-inch) seam allowance for both sides of this strip in your calculations.

3. Fold the strip in half lengthwise, then again widthwise.

4. Cutting along the four raw edges, turn this folded piece of fabric into a wedge shape (see illustration). It must be at least 1.5 cm (½ inch) wide at the narrow point when folded.

When you open it out it should look like a butterfly with very long wings. The narrow part in the middle must be at least 2.5 cm (1 inch) wide.

5. Line up the narrow part with the inseams of the sleeves and sew this strip in place, right sides together.

6. An alternative to inserting a gusset is to pick off the cuffs and insert a strip up the side of each leg, then reapply the cuff. In this case you may want to use the same fabric for your sleeves and collar that you use for your side strips.

If the cuffs of the shirt are in rough shape, simply apply stretch cuffs. These can also match the side insert.

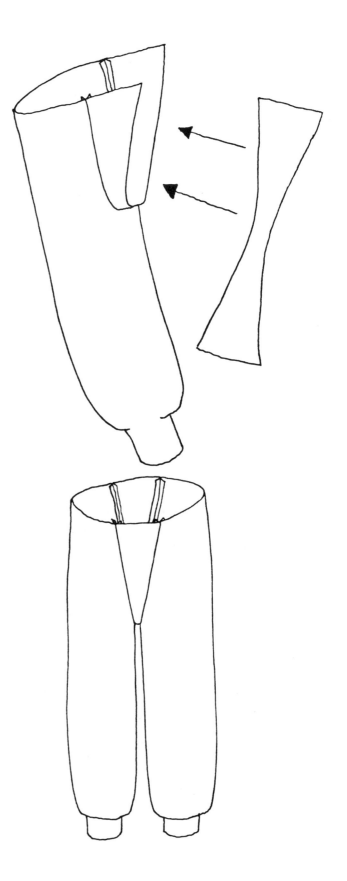

Adult Shirt Too Narrow

For a fuller tunic or top, before sewing the side seams, put a wide strip of fabric down either side, then gather the underarms to fit.

For a smart finish, you can pick the pockets off the shirt front and sew them over the inserts, midway down the sides.

Adult Sleeves Too Short

1. If the sleeves are too short for pants, try knickers instead (pants that finish just below the knee).

If you really must have pants from this shirt, you can get more length, depending on how much you need, by a variety of methods.

2. If the shirt cuff is quite short, and you only need a bit of extra length, replace it with a longer, ribbed or stretch-cotton cuff.

3. You might try cutting the bottom half of the sleeves off to attach a band of some tougher fabric. Make sure the band will cover the knee and that both bands are the same width. Reattach the ends of the sleeves, being sure that the button sides of the cuffs are both facing the back of the pants.

4. If the sleeves are really short you might consider making bloomers or shorts instead.

Collars

Collars can come from a variety of sources.

1. The easiest is to use the original shirt collar. Remember, though, that this collar will, in most cases, be loose on a child.

You can also cut off a badly frayed top collar but retain the base.

2. You can create your own bias tape for necklines and armholes with strips of scrap from the shirt. For a little extra touch, apply the bias tape over some lace cut off an old slip or nightgown. If there isn't enough shirt for bias scraps, rummage through your remnant box for some suitable fabric or ribbon.

3. You can rescue the collar off an old dress that has been badly stained or torn.

4. Bright stretch cotton is delightful for a turtleneck and sleeves. Often you can rescue a ready-made collar and sleeves from a shirt that has been ruined with the traces of many meals down the front.

Cut off the collar, as it has probably escaped the worst of the damage. Cut off the sleeves as well, to apply to the top you're designing, but remove the cuffs. They're usually pretty badly stained too.

Make new cuffs from the back of the shirt. Just lay open the original cuffs you just cut off and use them for a pattern. Remember to add seam allowance. Then apply the new cuffs to the original sleeves and insert the sleeves into the top.

Suggestions

1. Replace the sedate original shirt buttons with bright ones, matching or otherwise.

2. Hems can be as easy or fancy as you want.

You can use the existing shirt tails or hem.

You can attach a ruffle of scraps or contrasting fabric just under the hem.

You can sew in a multicoloured, multilayered petticoat, or a wide, gathered band of white eyelet lace.

Whatever choices you make, get comfortable with the guides. Give your imagination free reign. Don't get too complicated until you're sure of your own abilities and the use of the guides. Otherwise you may frustrate yourself out of completing an outfit.

If you're a parent, sewing with small children near or around, you can only count on a few minutes of concentrated effort at a time. Pace yourself and keep it simple. That way it's fun too.

CHAPTER SIX

Shirts to Rompers and Sunsuits

Designing and making children's rompers or sunsuits from adult shirts

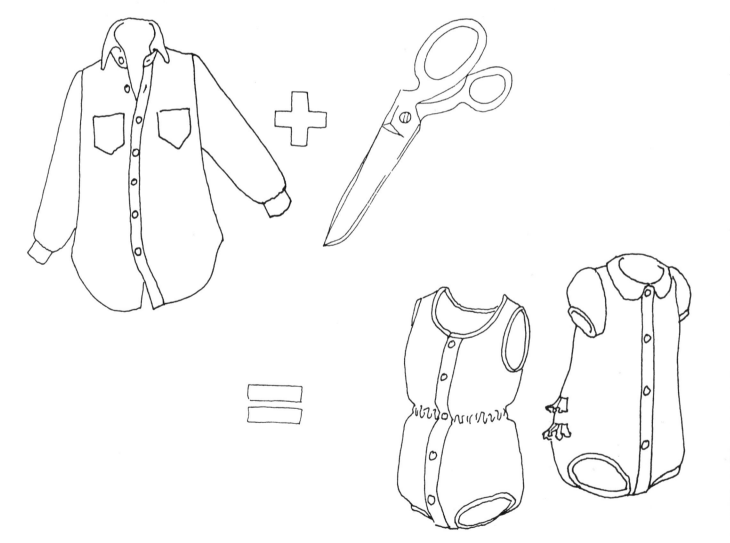

1. Measure

1. Measure your child according to the diagram.

2. Measure the body of the shirt you plan on using. Is it long enough to extend beyond the child's full body measurement?

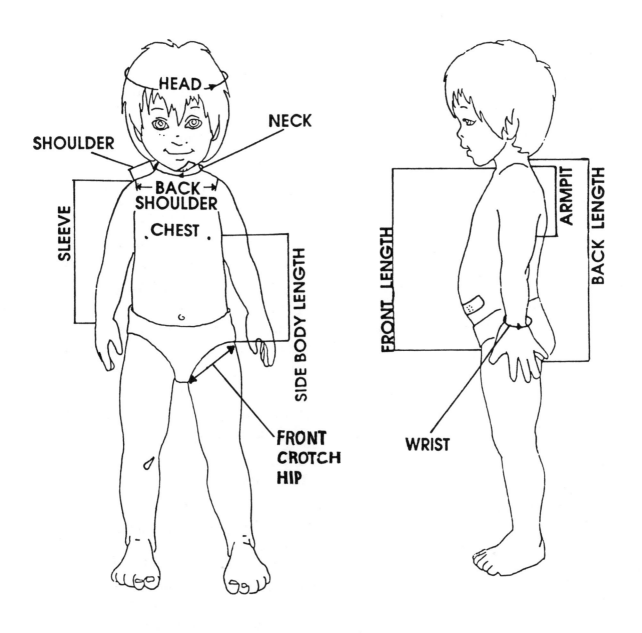

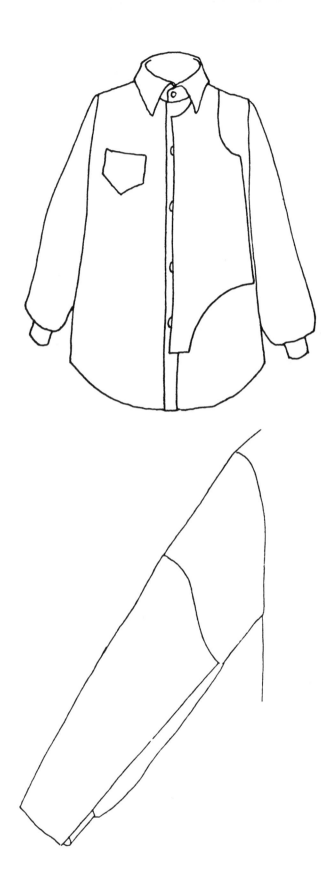

2. Mark

✂ **IF YOU'VE MADE A PATTERN** *(see page 122)*

1. Place the sleeve pattern on the sleeve of the adult shirt. If you plan on using the original cuff, be sure to place the cuff end of the pattern at the edge of the adult cuff. Line up the top or long edge of the sleeve pattern with the same edge of the shirt sleeve. Trace the pattern with dressmaker's chalk or any washable pencil.

2. If you don't plan on using the adult cuff, place the pattern at the shoulder end of the adult sleeve. This will also give you a fuller sleeve in the child's garment.

Cut the sleeve, *double thickness.*

3. Place the romper front pattern piece on the shirt front, being sure that the pattern centre is lined up with the centre of the shirt front If you plan on using the original shirt collar, place the shoulders of the pattern on the shoulders of the adult shirt.

If you want to create a new collar, place the front pattern piece so that the neckline lies 4 cm (1 1/2 inches) above a button. This will make finishing the collar much simpler, as you will already have a button and buttonhole in place.

4. Flip the shirt and repeat step 3, using the back pattern piece.

5. Cut the shirt out as marked, *single thickness.*

✂ **IF YOU HAVEN'T MADE A PATTERN**

Select guides **E, F, G, H,** and **J.**

1. If you're using the original shirt collar, mark the centre line of the shirt front and shirt back (just below the collar) and then smooth the shirt out flat, face up.

2. From the centre mark, measure out half of the child's shoulder back measurement, first in one direction and then in the other.

3. Place the armpit guide **G** at this point, first on one side, then the other. Flip the shirt and repeat for the back of the adult garment. The back shoulder measurement is applied to both the front and the back of the adult garment to ensure that the armpit guides will line up from front to back. It also allows greater freedom of movement in the finished child's garment.

4. If you're creating a new neckline, you still need to mark the centre line of the shirt, front and back. Once this is done, place the neck guide **E**, as high as you can, on the centre lines, both front and back. The back neck guide should lie about 5 cm (2 inches) higher than the front neck guide.

5. Measure out, at a slight downward angle, on either side of the neck curve, your desired shoulder width, plus 2.5 cm (1 inch) for seam allowance. Mark these lines clearly.

6. Place the armpit guide **G** at the ends of these lines.

7. If you want more fullness to the playsuit body, angle the armpit guide **G** right out to both sides of the shirt. Be careful to avoid catching the sleeves in the armpit curves. Trace the curves.

8. Measure down from the base of the armpit curve your desired side body length, plus about 8 cm (3 inches). Mark this point.

9. Measure down the shirt front your desired front body length, plus about 8 cm (3 inches). Mark this point.

10. Place the front crotch-hip guide **H** at the bottom of the centre line. Angle the guide so that the hip point of the guide comes to the desired side body point. Flip the guide and repeat for the other leg.

11. If the shirt is too wide for the guide at this point, merely extend the line of the

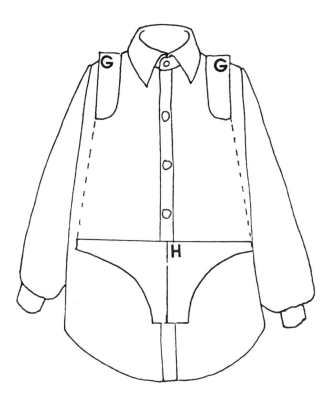

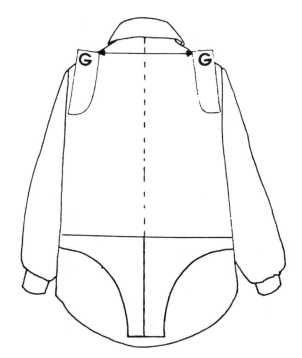

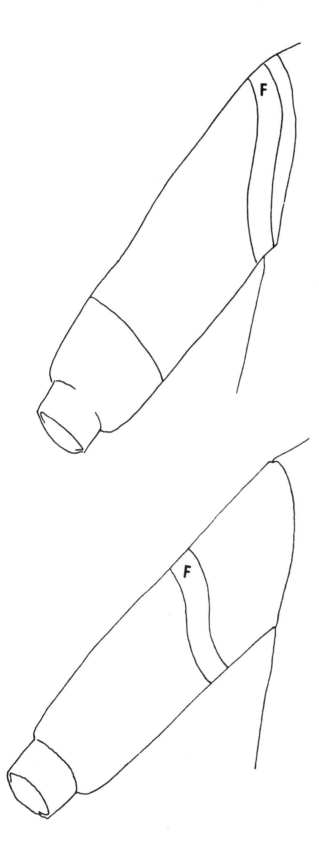

guide out until it meets the desired side point of the shirt. When you come to sew the outfit, the gathering will just be a little fuller at this point.

12. If the shirt is too narrow for the guide, and moving the guide up just a little doesn't solve the problem, relax. There's a solution. Turn to **NOTES**.

13. If the shirt front is marked like the diagram, then turn the garment over and smooth it flat. Make sure the armpit and hip marks from the front are extended a bit around to the back so you can use them to place your back guides. Repeat steps 1 through 11, using the back neck guide **E** and back crotch guide **J** and the back body length measurement.

14. Cut the shirt out *single thickness.*

15. If you're planning on sleeves, you can measure your sleeve length from the shoulder of the adult sleeve down for a full sleeve. In this case, first place and trace the sleeve guide **F** at the top of the sleeve, as shown, and measure down the desired sleeve length. Cut off the bottom part and cut the top, *double thickness,* along the curve you've already traced there.

16. If you wish to use the cuff from the adult shirt, measure up from the cuff. Place your sleeve guides at this point and trace the curves. Once again, cut *double thickness.*

17. Cut two lengths of .5-cm (¼-inch) elastic to match your child's upper leg measurement.

Have a cup of coffee and then let your toddler out of the high chair, crib, or playpen for a break.

3. Make

1. If you're using the original collar, sew your side seams.

2. Fold an edge over to the inside of the garment along the leg-hole curve and then fold it over again. Sew this to form a casing for the elastic. Make sure the two crotch ends are the same width.

3. Thread the elastic through the casings and secure the ends.

4. Fold an edge under on the crotch flaps, then fold them under again and sew, being sure to secure the elastic ends in the line of stitching. It's a good idea to cover the elastic ends with a double or triple line of stitching at this point, to be sure that it's secure.

5. Attach three snaps, by applicator, or the sewn-in variety, across the ends of the crotch flaps. Snaps are easier than buttons, particularly for children over the age of two. Make sure they are securely attached, as they'll be subjected to a lot of wear and tear.

6. Insert the sleeves, making sure the underarm seams are lined up with the side seams. Sometimes, depending on the width of the original adult sleeves, they won't fit perfectly into the armholes of the child's garment.

If the sleeve is too large, simply gather it a little at the shoulder.

If the sleeve is too small for the shirt, but is perfect for the child, you can tighten up the armhole a little by angling the shoulder seam down towards the armhole at a steeper angle. If the armhole is still too large, bring the side seams in a little too, making sure to move both sides in the same amount.

7. If you're using the cuffs on the original sleeves, be very careful that you place them

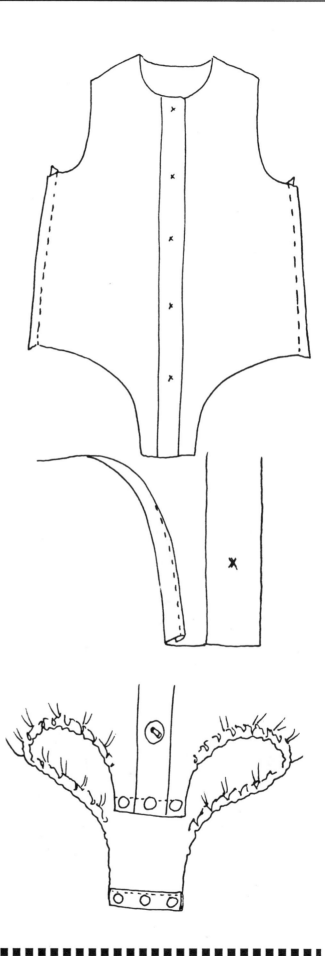

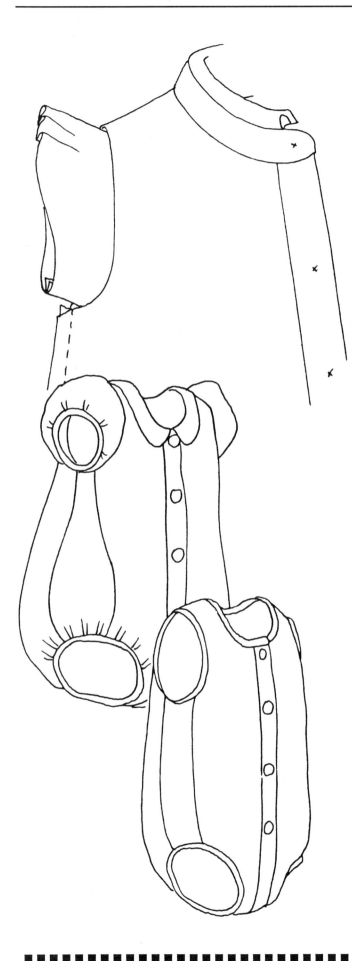

into the armholes so that the cuffs open towards the back of the sleeves.

8. If you're putting in a gathered cuff, measure the elastic to fit your child's wrist and make your casing on the inside of the sleeve. For a ruffled cuff, put the elastic casing about 6 cm (2 1/2 inches) back from the end of the sleeve. Hem the cuff.

9. If you're creating your own new neckline, sew the shoulder seams and finish the neck by whatever means you have devised. See **NOTES** if you need some ideas here.

Once the neckline is established and the shoulder seams sewn, simply continue from step 1 through the **MAKE** instructions.

4. Notes

Adult Shirt Too Narrow

If the shirt is too narrow to accommodate your child's hips and thighs, all is not lost.

1. Find a fabric scrap that is the same weight as the shirt and a colour that works well with it. Cut two strips a bit longer than the garment's side seams. Cut these strips wide enough to enlarge the suit to fit nicely. Make sure the strips are the same width and sew them into the side seams.

For a little extra pizzaz, you might try putting in tapered strips (the wide end is at the playsuit leg).

2. Use scraps of the same fabric to make bias tape for the neck and leg openings of the outfit. (This is a bright alternative to a folded-under casing.) If you're making a sleeveless playsuit, trim the armholes with the same bias tape.

Adult Shirt Too Short

1. If the shirt is too short, you can make a two-tone playsuit. Cut out and make the playsuit, leaving it too short. Then cut the playsuit in half at the waist and sew in a band of contrasting, matching or complementing fabric.

2. Now sew the bottom back on. Make sure the bottom is facing the same way as the top when you do this. An extra touch, in this case, would be to sew a casing into this colour band and make the playsuit elastic-waisted.

3. A variation on this same theme is to use a sturdy stretch material for the colour band. However, instead of cutting the stretch material to fit the playsuit, cut it to fit the child's waist. Then gather the playsuit to fit the band as you sew the two together.

Alternative Necklines

1. The base of the original shirt collar works quite nicely for a larger child.

2. For an added touch, open up the top of the collar base and insert some lace. Then restitch the collar base.

3. If you cut the original collar right off, you end up with an open neckline. If it's not too full a neckline for your child, finish it with bias tape and/or lace.

4. You may find that some of the little collars, either from your fabric store or off an old dress, work very nicely too. If the neckline is too full, gather it before you add your collar.

5. You can save the neck and sleeves from an old cotton turtleneck with a badly stained front. Before you sew in the turtleneck, make sure the neckline of the shirt will fit over the child's head. Then simply sew the turtleneck on, right sides together. Insert the sleeves as described earlier in the instructions.

6. For a sunsuit you may want fastenable shoulder straps. In this case, extend the shoulders up, about 4 cm (1½ inches) for the front and about 7 cm (3 inches) for the

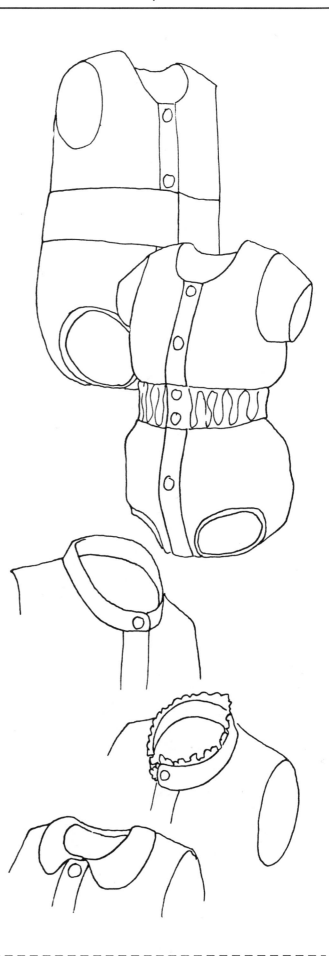

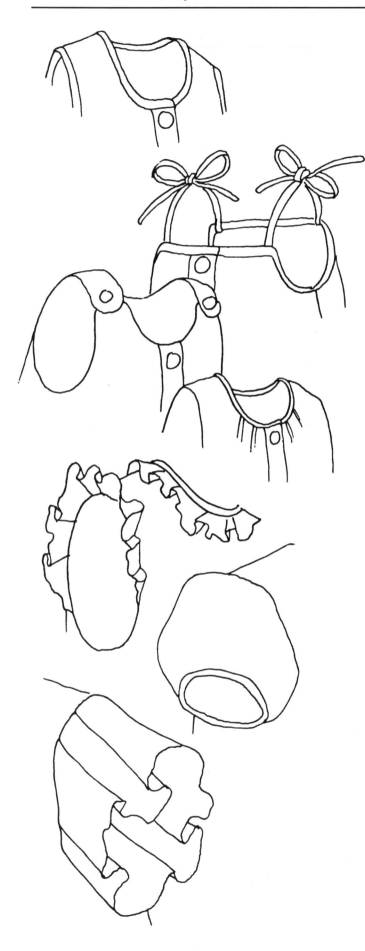

back. Round the ends of the shoulder straps and finish them as you would the neckline. If you plan on using buttons, put the buttonholes in the ends of the back straps.

7. If there's not enough room in the shirt for fastenable shoulder straps, cut the shirt straight across at the top. Don't even bother with a neckline.

Gather and finish the edge with bias tape and use some more bias tape to make tie shoulder strings.

Alternative Sleeves

1. Use just the top of the original sleeve to make a short puffy sleeve on the rompers. This sleeve can be open and loose, maybe finished with lace, or you can close it with elastic. Measure the upper arm for the elastic and add 2.5 cm (1 inch) to this amount. You don't want the elastic too tight here, as the flesh of the upper arm is quite tender.

2. You can also finish the armhole with a capped ruffle made from shirt scraps. Try lace and seam binding or piping.

3. If you want to have some easy fun, turn two shirts into rompers and swap the sleeves. In this case you may want to swap the collars too.

Alternative Leg Openings

1. The leg opening can be closed simply with a casing and elastic. For a little extra effort, you can cut a contrasting casing. If you have a serger, this can be applied very quickly and easily. Cut a length of bias tape wide enough to accommodate the elastic and a seam allowance when folded over. This bias tape must be the same length as the measurement along the edge of the leg opening.

Fold the tape in half lengthwise and, right sides together, serge it to the leg curve. If you're feeling very competent or just want to walk on the wild side, try to serge this folded strip on with the elastic already in it. Just be careful to not catch the elastic in the line of sewing.

It's a good idea to make sure that the starting end of the elastic is secured as well, or the whole thing will just pull through as you stretch it to sew the casing. Then you'll have to fish the elastic out and thread it through anyway.

2. For a younger female child, it's fun to finish the leg with lace.

3. If you want to try something a little different, especially if you've put a ribbed waist in the garment, cut 7-cm-wide (3-inch) strips of ribbing that fit the top of the child's leg. Fold these strips lengthwise and stretch them to fit the leg edge as you sew them, right sides together. To really finish this look off nicely, try using the same stretch material for the neck and sleeves. When you use the stretch material for the legs, you may want to finish the crotch flaps with bias tape, otherwise the flap may be too bulky. It depends on the weight of the stretch fabric.

This particular outfit is especially practical as an alternative to dresses for crawling babies. You can make them as ruffly as you want, even adding a couple of rows of ruffles across the bottom. The resulting outfit is pretty, but comfortable and functional. If you cut it large enough, the child can wear it under a skirt or jumper next year. If you take the ruffles off, it'll even fit under jeans. If it gets too short in the body before it gets too small anywhere else, just cut the crotch flaps off and refinish the bottom edge as a shirt.

Whether you're making a sunsuit, or rompers, or simply a shirt that will stay tucked in, remember to build in the options you want, use your imagination and have fun.

CHAPTER SEVEN

Sweaters to Tops and Overalls

Designing and making children's tops and overalls or pants from adult sweaters

This information is more successfully applied with the use of a serger or an overlock stitch to prevent fraying of knitted material.

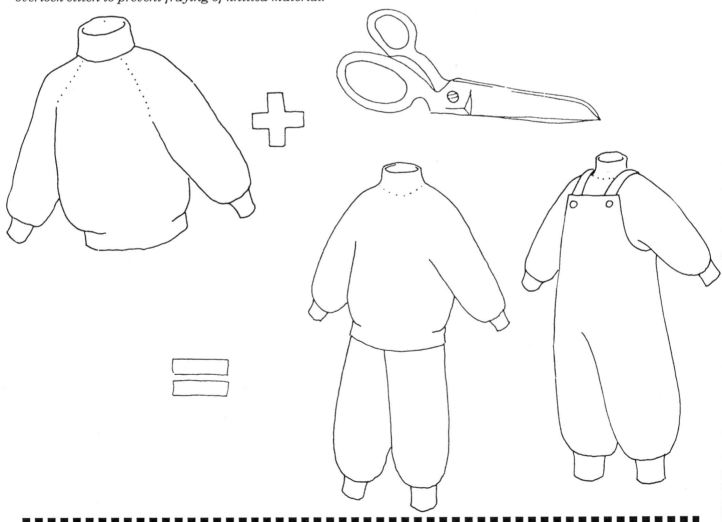

1. Measure

1. Measure your child according to the diagram.

If you're working with a very tiny child, you may want to do this when the child is sleeping or you are particularly rested. An extra pair of hands helps too.

2. Measure the length of the adult sweater sleeve to be sure that it's long enough to accommodate the child's combined full body and inseam measurements.

3. Check the sleeve width to be sure that it's wide enough to fit your child's hips and tummy after it's been converted to overalls.

To do this, measure the circumference of the adult sleeve at the armpit point. Now subtract 6 cm (2 1/2 inches). Multiply this number by two. If the final figure is smaller than your child's hips or waist measurement, this sweater had better be very stretchy or the pants aren't going to fit. If it looks like it's going to be a tight fit, turn to **NOTES** for help.

4. If you are working with a crew-necked sweater, measure the neck to see if it's big enough to accommodate your child's hips. If it is you can use this sweater upside down. (See **MARK**.)

5. Measure the body width of the adult sweater and double it. Now add the child's chest measurement and the upper arm circumferences (that's both arms). If the child's chest and arm measurement is greater than the doubled measurement of the adult sweater body, you may have to make a vest or a short-sleeved top.

See **NOTES** for help with this.

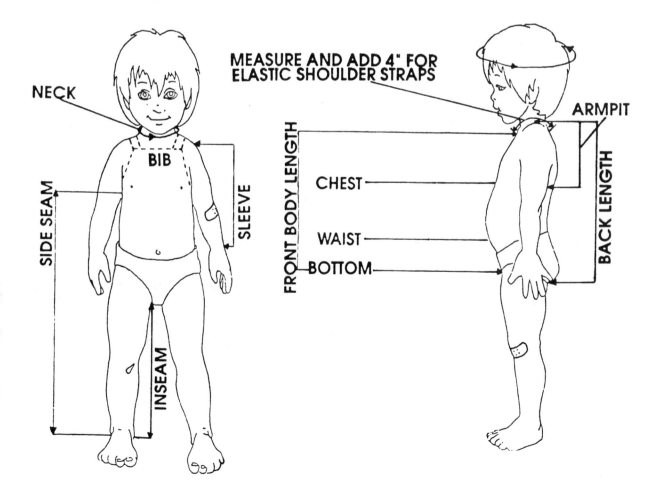

NECK

MEASURE AND ADD 4" FOR ELASTIC SHOULDER STRAPS

BIB

SIDE SEAM

SLEEVE

INSEAM

FRONT BODY LENGTH

CHEST

WAIST

BOTTOM

ARMPIT

BACK LENGTH

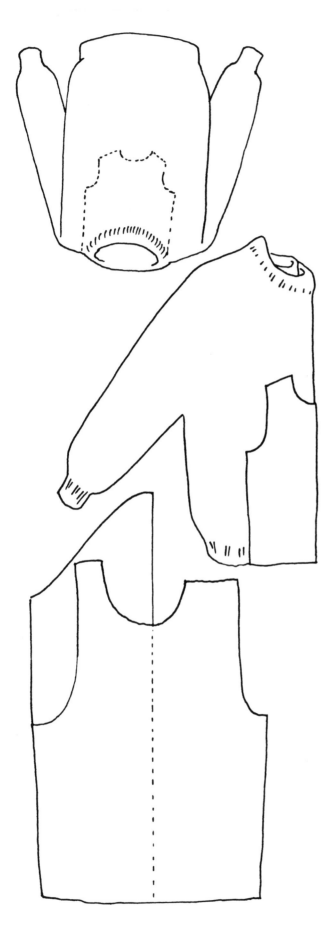

2. Mark

✂ **IF YOU'VE MADE PATTERNS** *(see page 115, 116)*

Overalls

1. Place the front crotch inseam line of the pants or overalls pattern along the underarm seam of one sleeve. If the centre line of the pattern is well outside the other edge of the sleeve, the sleeve is too narrow for pants or overalls. Turn to **NOTES** for suggestions.

If the centre line of the pattern lies well within the edge of the adult sleeve, make the inseam a little longer to allow for a baggier garment that will fit the child for a longer period of time.

Trace the pattern with dressmaker's chalk or a washable marker.

2. Flip the sweater and repeat step 1 using the back half of the overalls or pants pattern.

3. Cut out the pants or overalls, being careful to cut *single thickness*.

Sweater

1. Lay the adult sweater face up and place the back top pattern piece in the centre front, lining up the bottom edge of the pattern with the finished bottom edge of the adult sweater. Trace the pattern.

2. Trace the sleeve pattern, first on one side of the marked top back, then the other. Once again, be sure to place the cuff end of the pattern on the edge of the finished, bottom edge of the adult sweater.

3. Cut everything out as marked, *double thickness*.

4. Once the sweater has been cut out take the first of the two top pieces and smooth it out. Lay the top front pattern piece evenly on this cut-out piece of the sweater. It should be a perfect match everywhere but at the neck. The front neck should be cut 5 cm (2 inches) deeper than the back neck. Trace the front neckline and cut it out.

✂ IF YOU HAVEN'T MADE PATTERNS

Select guides **A, B, C, D, E, F** and **G**.

Overalls

1. Smooth out the sweater, face up.

2. Measure up the underarm seam of the sleeve the desired inseam length.

3. Place the front crotch guide **B** at this point.

4. Trace the curve. Make sure you can see the end of this line from the other side of the sleeve.

5. Extend the front crotch line up to the desired front body height and clearly mark the top point.

6. Draw a line at right angles to this, towards the other side of the sleeve. Mark this line off at half the desired front bib width, plus 2.5 cm (1 inch) for seam allowance.

7. Place the front armpit guide **D** at this point so that the curve extends down and out towards the other edge of the sleeve.

8. Trace the curve.

9. If the curve ends a little short of the edge of the sleeve, extend it until it touches the side. Make sure you can see the end of this line from the other side of the sleeve.

10. Repeat for the other sleeve.

11. Flip the sweater and smooth it out again.

12. Repeat steps 2 through 10, using the back crotch guide **A** and the back overall armpit guide **C**. Make sure the back crotch points and armpit points match up with those on the front.

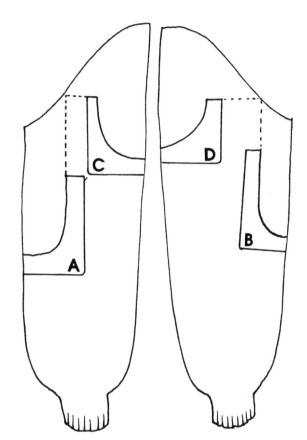

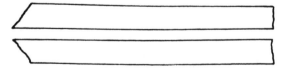

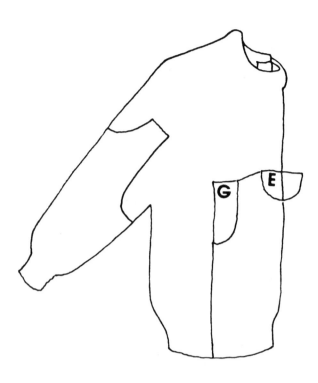

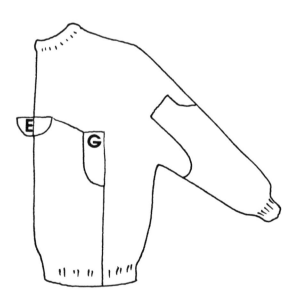

13. Cut the sleeves, *single thickness*.

14. Cut two lengths of 2.5-cm (1-inch) elastic to match the child's shoulder strap measurement plus 10 cm (4 inches). Cut one end of each strap at about a 45-degree angle. This will make it easier to insert the straps at the same angle.

Top

1. Fold the sweater in half as evenly as possible, with the front of the sweater on the inside.

2. Measure out, at a right angle from the centre fold, one-quarter of the child's chest measurement plus about 2.5 cm (1 inch) for seam allowance.

3. Extend this line up from the bottom of the sweater, keeping it parallel to the fold.

4. Mark off the desired side measurement on this line. Trace the line.

5. Place the armpit guide **G** at the top of this line.

6. Measure up the fold from the bottom of the sweater your desired back length.

7. Place the back neck guide **E** at this point, being careful to keep the centre line of the guide on the fold of the sweater.

8. Measure out from the edge of the neck guide **E** your desired shoulder width plus about 2.5 cm (1 inch) to allow for seam allowances. If possible, use a ruler for this measurement.

9. Move the shoulder line up or down until it touches the top of the armpit guide **G**. This should give you a slight down-sloping angle to the shoulder line.

Trace the shoulder line.

10. Trace the neck curve and the armhole curve.

11. Open the sweater out flat and cut, *single thickness,* the half of the back that you've marked.

12. Fold over the cut half of the back and use it as a pattern for the other half.

13. Cut the rest of the back out, *single thickness.*

14. Fold the front of the sweater in half, being careful to match up the side seams.

15. Repeat steps 2 through 13, using the front neck guide and the front body measurement.

16. Lay the remains of the adult sweater flat.

17. Extend the straight edge, where the side of the child's sweater body was cut out, up from the bottom edge of the adult garment, until it matches your desired sleeve length.

18. Place the shoulder end of the sleeve guide **F** at this point, with the armpit end at the side seam of the adult sweater. Trace the guide.

19. Repeat for the other side and cut out both sleeves, *double thickness.*

20. From the scraps of the sweater cut a strip that will stretch long enough to fit around the child's head, plus about 2.5 cm (1 inch).

This strip could be anywhere from 8 to 30 cm (3 to 12 inches) wide, depending on the neck style you've chosen for the child's top. It also depends on the amount of scrap available. If there just isn't enough sweater left to make a neck, refer to **NOTES** for some alternative necklines.

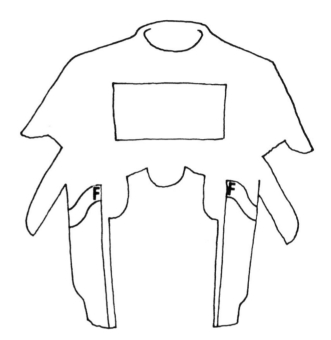

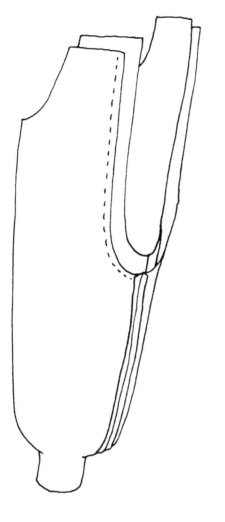

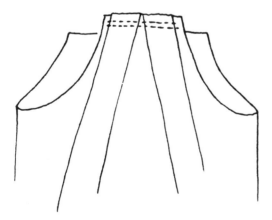

3. Make

Overalls

1. Turn one sleeve inside out.

2. Slip the other sleeve inside the one that's inside out. Make sure the inseams are lined up.

3. Sew the two sleeves together along the large U-shaped edge.

4. Turn the pants (that's what they just became) right side out.

5. Serge the top edges of the bibs and armpits, or finish with bias tape. If you're using bias tape, remember that it won't be stretchy like the sweater. This can help the overalls retain their shape at the top. If they were going to be a tight fit, though, this may make them impossible for the child to put on.

6. Attach the shoulder straps at the top of the back bib.

7. Snaps do not work well with knit fabric unless you decide to face the bibs instead of folding the edge or finishing with bias tape. (See **NOTES**.)

Suspender clips work well and can be bought new or taken from an old pair of suspenders. If you use buttons, be sure to reinforce the buttonholes. They'll stretch if you don't.

This might be a good time to take a break. On the other hand, the thought of being finished in about fifteen minutes could be enough to keep you going.

Top

1. Sew the shoulder seams, right sides together.

2. Sew the side seams, right sides together.

3. Sew the top seam of each sleeve, right sides together.

4. Insert the sleeves, being careful to line up the underarm seams of the sleeves with the side seams of the top. Sew, you guessed it, right sides together.

5. Make a tube of the strip you cut for the neck.

6. Fold the tube over on itself so that the right side shows. This means that the tube is now half as deep as it was, but the raw edges of the seam are hidden and the tube is double thickness.

7. Turn the sweater inside out and insert the tube into the neck opening. Keep the seam of the tube to the back of the neck.

8. Stretch the tube to fit the neck as you sew the two together. Be careful to catch all three layers of raw edge when you sew.

Now you can take a break. Unless you want to see if the outfit fits.

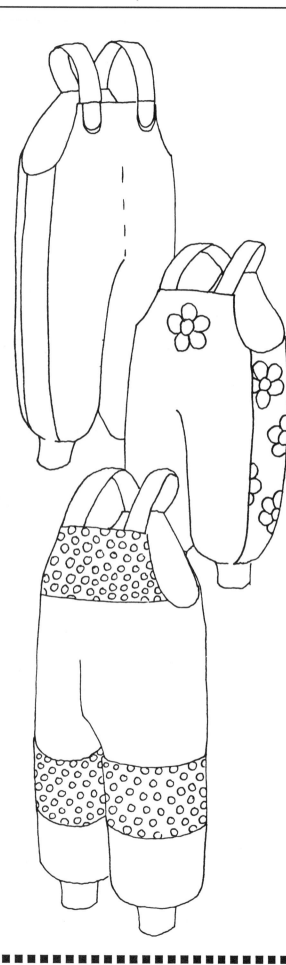

4. Notes

Adult Sleeves Too Narrow

This is not likely to be the case unless the sleeves are too short as well. In the rare instance where it does apply, however, there is a solution.

1. Cut out the overalls, even though they are too narrow.

2. Cut open the sides of the overalls and sew in a fabric strip that suits the knit of the sweater being transformed. This insert can be stretch material, but it can just as easily be any other material. If the fabric content of the strips is uncertain, try to preshrink them by washing and drying them. This only applies with strips of new material.

Try to use the same fabric for bias tape to finish the top of the overall. If there's enough of this fabric, try it for a pocket or an appliqué on the front bib.

Adult Sleeves Too Short

1. If the sleeves are plenty wide enough, but too short, before marking the guides or pattern, measure the distance from the child's ankle to just below the knee.

2. Mark this measurement on the sleeve, measuring up from the cuff.

3. Cut the sleeve off at this point and sew in a tube the same circumference as the sleeve. Make sure the tube is deep enough to give you the length you need for the overalls. This tube is a good idea at the knee, because you can choose a bright tough fabric. This way you can enhance the colour or design of the sweater and protect the knees of the child and the garment at the same time. Try some of the same fabric for elbow patches.

4. If you don't want tough fabric, use sections from the sleeves of another sweater.

5. You can also use bits of another sweater, (or the one the sleeves are from) to make the bibs of the overall.

6. If the sleeves are just a bit too short, try a shorter bib with longer straps.

7. Another way to lengthen a sleeve that's just a smidgen too short is to sew cuffs onto the original sweater cuffs.

Adult Sleeves Too Wide

It won't happen.

Adult Sweater Body Too Narrow

If the sweater body is too narrow for the child's sweater body and sleeves, you have a few alternatives.

1. Make a capped sleeve top by curving the tops of the armpit guides out.

2. Make a vest instead of a sweater.

3. Use a light fabric to make sleeves or cut the sleeves off a shirt that is badly stained elsewhere.

To make sleeves of new material, fold the fabric and place the shoulder end of the sleeve guide at the fold. Measure the desired sleeve length along the fold. Then, at right angles to the fold, measure out the child's wrist circumference. Connect the end of the wrist line with the armpit point of the sleeve guide.

To create the second sleeve, either place the folded first sleeve on the fold and trace it out, or open it and the fabric out and trace and cut the single thickness. In the case of cutting single thickness, make sure the right sides are together. A nice finish for a cotton sleeve is a cuff made from sweater scraps.

4. Cut up another sweater to make sleeves.

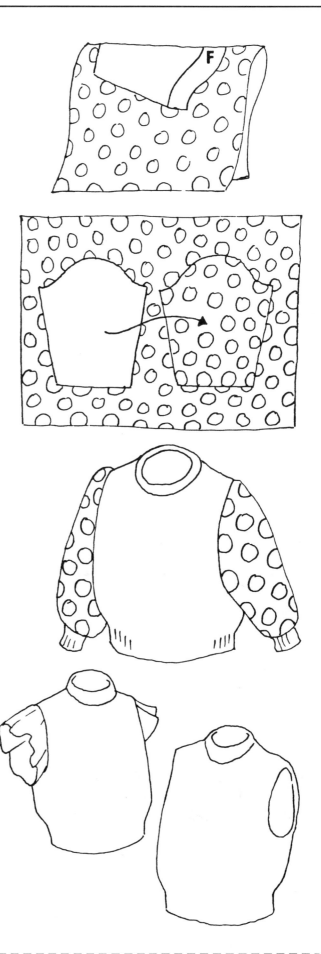

■■■

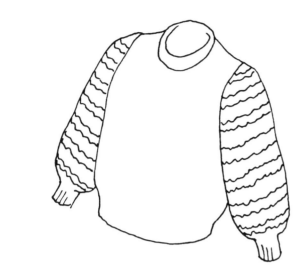

Alternative Necklines

1. If there just isn't enough sweater to make a neckline, either buy some ribbed fabric or steal the cuffs off another garment that didn't need them anyway.

If you've been reduced to cuff pilfering, cut the two cuffs open and then sew them together again to make a tube large enough for a child's head to fit through. Apply this tube as you would the turtleneck described earlier.

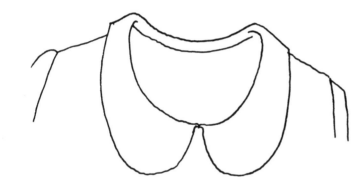

2. If you're above cuff theft, but short on cash or time, simply serge and then roll the neck opening.

If you have no serger, make sure the neck opening will fit the child's head and finish it with bias tape. If the outfit is for a girl, a bit of lace under the bias tape is a nice touch too.

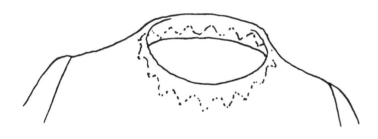

3. If the neck opening is large enough to accommodate the child's head, you can finish it with any non-stretchy material at your disposal. This includes ready-made collars and collars taken from old dresses or shirts.

Experiment a little. The raw materials you're working with can always be turned into something else if you make any serious mistakes. If you think about it, you can't really make mistakes with Short Kutz. If something doesn't work, the fabric hasn't been wasted. So live a little, take a walk on the wild side and have fun.

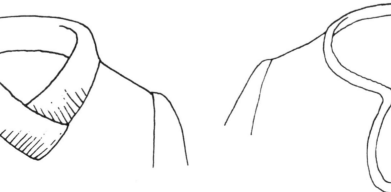

CHAPTER EIGHT

Sweaters to Dresses and Pants

Designing and making
children's dresses
and leggings or tunics
and pants from
adult sweaters

This information is more successfully applied with the use of a serger or an overlock stitch.

1. Measure

1. Measure your child according to the diagram. You may want to add 2.5 to 5 cm (1 or 2 inches) to the sleeve and leg measurements to allow for growth.

2. Measure the sweater sleeve to be sure that it's long enough to accommodate your child's full outside pant seam length. Add 4 cm (1½ inches) to this measurement for a waistband. If the sleeves are too short, refer to **NOTES**. Check the width of the sleeve. If the sum of the circumferences of both sleeves, minus 28 cm (11 inches), is less than your child's hips, the sleeves are too narrow for pants. If this is the case, refer to **NOTES** for suggestions.

3. Measure the width of the sweater body and multiply by two. If this amount is greater than the sum of your child's chest and upper arm measurements, then you can make a full top. If the adult sweater is too narrow, you'll have to be content with a tunic-style top or vest.

4. Measure the length of the adult sweater body. Is it long enough to accommodate your child's full dress length? It can't be too long, but it can be too short. If the latter is the case, refer to **NOTES** for suggestions.

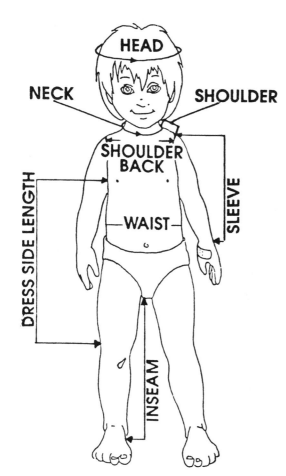

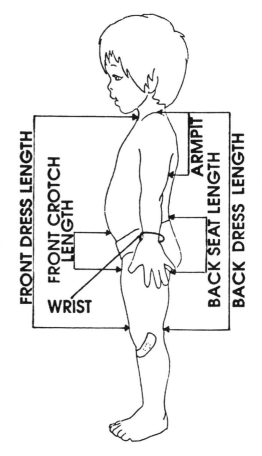

2. Mark

✂ **IF YOU'VE MADE PATTERNS** *(see pages 115, 119)*

Pants

1. Smooth the adult sweater out flat, face up. Place the front inseam of the pants pattern along the underarm seam of the sleeve. Be sure that the cuff end of the pattern is at the edge of the sweater cuff. If the centre line of the pattern lies well beyond the outer sleeve edge, the sleeve is too narrow to transform into pants. See **NOTES** for help with this.

2. If the centre line of the pattern is well within the edge of the sleeve, you can make baggy pants. If this is the case, you may want to make the pants a little longer too. That way they might fit next year too. Trace the pattern with dressmaker's chalk or a washable marker.

3. Flip the sweater, smooth it out and repeat steps 1 and 2 using the back inseam of the pants pattern.

4. Cut the sweater as marked, *single thickness*.

Dress

1. Smooth the adult sweater out, face up, and place the dress front pattern on the front, being careful to line up the centre line of the pattern with the centre of the sweater. If you're planning to use the original sweater collar, place the shoulders of the pattern on the shoulders of the sweater and only mark the armpits and side seams. If you don't plan to use the original collar, place the front pattern piece so that the hem edge is flush with the bottom finished edge of the adult sweater. Trace the pattern.

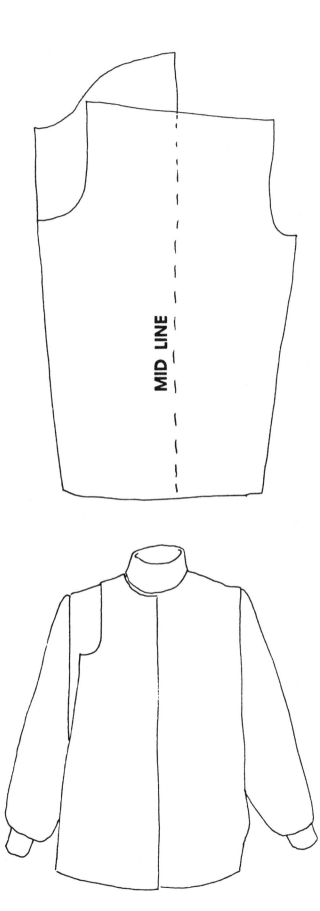

MID LINE

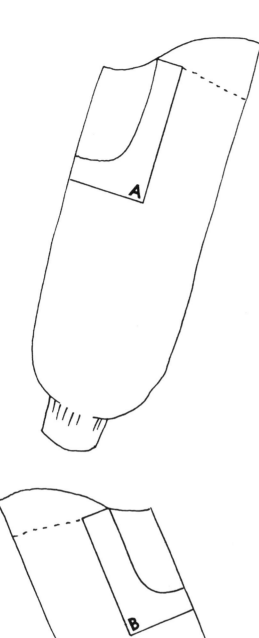

2. Flip the sweater and repeat step 1 using the back dress pattern piece.

3. Cut the sweater as marked, *single thickness.*

✂ **IF YOU HAVEN'T MADE PATTERNS**

Select guides **A**, **B**, **E**, **F** and **G**.

Pants

1. Smooth the sweater out, right side up. Measure along the underarm seam of the sleeve, from the cuff, your desired inseam length. You may want to add about 5 cm (2 inches) for growth and activity.

2. Place the front crotch guide **B** at this point and trace the curve. Add 5 cm (2 inches) to this line to allow for the waistband.

3. Repeat for the other sleeve.

4. Cut a length of 2-cm (3/4-inch) elastic 1 cm (1/2 inch) or so shorter than the child's waist measurement.

5. Flip the sweater and repeat the above steps on the sleeve backs, this time using the back crotch guide **A**. Be sure to match your inseam points with those marked on the front of the sleeves.

6. Draw a line on each sleeve connecting the front crotch line with the back crotch line.

There is likely to be a slight angle to this line, rising towards the back. This is normal as the seat of any pair of pants tends to rise higher than the front.

If you wish to allow extra room for movement, you might even want to raise the back waistband a little bit higher than your measurements would indicate. This is particularly true if your child is still in diapers.

7. Cut each sleeve as marked, *single thickness.*

Dress

1. Turn the sweater face up again.

2. If you are using the original collar, measure out, from the centre neck point, half the desired shoulder back width in each direction. If you're not using the original collar, go on to step 7.

3. Place the armpit guide **G** at this point on either side.

4. Trace the curves.

5. From the bottom point of the armpit curves, draw a line out to the side of the sweater. Angle this line out so that it smoothly joins the side seam of the sweater.

6. Cut the side seams and armpits *double thickness*.

7. If you are not planning on using the neck of the original sweater, measure up the side seams your desired side dress length.

8. Place your armpit guide **G** on each side of the sweater at this point.

9. Measure up the sweater centre front your desired dress front length.

10. Place your front neck guide **E** at the top of this line. Be sure to centre the guide with the centre line.

11. Trace your guides and connect the top points to form your shoulders. If the shoulder slopes towards the neck, move the neck guide **E** up until the slope is down towards the arm.

12. Flip the sweater and repeat the procedure on the back, using the back neck guide. Check to be sure that all your shoulder, neck and armpit points line up.

13. Cut the dress out of the sweater. In this case be sure to cut *single thickness*.

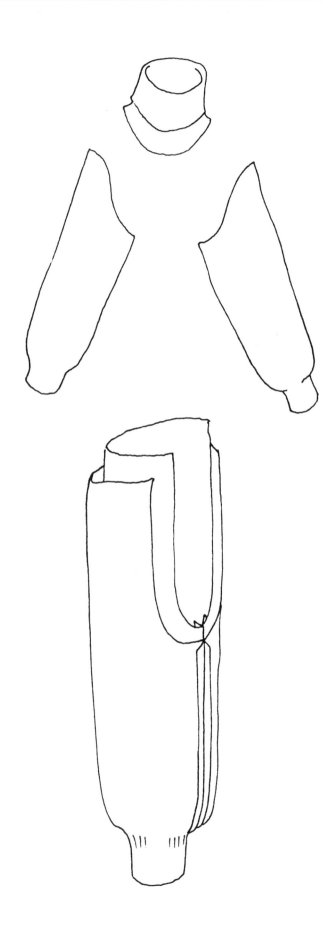

Sleeves (*optional*)

1. The sleeves from this sweater have already been cut to make trousers, but if you want sleeves for the top, you have several options.

2. Cut the sleeves and neck from an old turtleneck and use them to finish the top. Measure up the sleeves from the cuff the desired sleeve length and place the sleeve guide **F** at this point. Trace the curve. When you come to make the outfit, simply insert the turtleneck and sleeves into the sweater dress with the right sides together.

3. Use the sleeves from another sweater that complements the colours in the sweater you've used for the tunic and pants.

4. If you want to get really fancy, find two sweaters that go beautifully together. Use one sweater to make the pants, sleeves, and collar while you use the other one to make the body of the top.

3. Make

Pants

1. Turn one sleeve inside out.

2. Stick the sleeve that's right side out inside the one that's inside out.

3. Line up the front to the front and the back to the back.

4. Sew the U-shaped crotch seam and turn the pants right side out.

5. Serge or fold over .5 cm (1/4 inch) at the waistband, then fold the waistband over, about 2.5 cm (1 inch) for 2-cm (3/4-inch) elastic, and make a casing. Leave an opening about 2.5 cm (1 inch) wide in the edge of the casing.

6. Using a large safety pin, thread the elastic through the casing.

Be sure to pin the tail end in place before you pull the elastic all the way through, otherwise you really will pull it all the way through and have to start over again.

7. Sew the ends of the elastic together and slip the elastic completely into the casing.

8. Close the casing.

The pants are done. Honest.

Dress

1. If you are using the original sweater collar, sew the side seams.

2. If you're using sleeves, turn the top inside out. Put a right-side-out sleeve inside the top. Line the sleeve edge up with the armhole edge. Make sure, also, that the underarm seams are lined up and the right sides are together. Sew the sleeve in. Repeat for the other sleeve.

3. Now see if it fits.

4. If you're creating your own neckline, sew the shoulder seams.

5. Sew the side seams.

6. If you're using sleeves, refer back to step 2.

7. If you're using a turtleneck to finish the collar, line up the neck seam with the centre back and apply it the same way you did the sleeves. If you're not using a turtleneck, you can serge and roll the neck edge under, finish it with bias tape, or apply a collar from another dress. Remember, though, that if you are applying a non-stretchy neckline or collar, it must be openable or larger than the child's head.

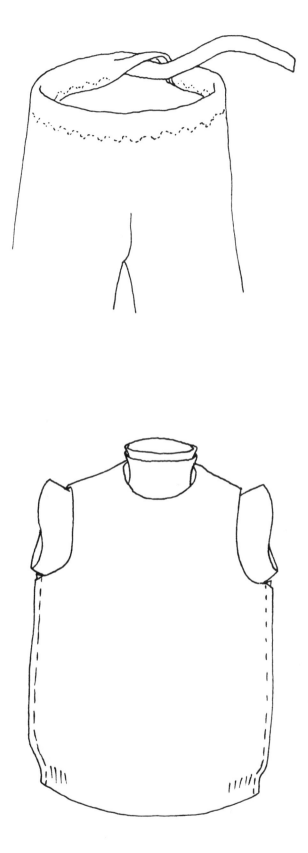

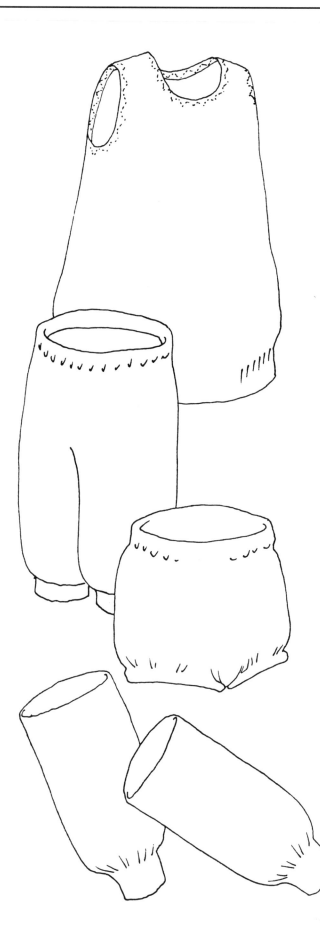

8. If you're not using sleeves, you can finish the armholes by serging the raw edge and then folding it under. Another option here is to finish the armholes with bias tape made from sweater or fabric scraps.

Voilà! You're done.

4. Notes

Adult Sleeves Too Short

If the sleeves of the adult garment are too short for full-length pants, you have a few options open to you.

1. Make knickers, shorts or bloomers, depending on how short the adult sleeves are. To do this, simply measure the inseam to suit knickers, shorts, or bloomers.

2. Make the trousers and then cut the legs off where the knees would be. Sew in a band (the same width for each leg) of sturdy fabric that will extend the pants to the desired length.

3. Make gaiters instead of pants, as shown. Finish the raw end of the sleeves with cuffing, store-bought or pinched from another sweater.

4. Make a wide waistband with some rib-knit or the bottom band of another sweater.

Adult Sleeves Too Narrow

If the sleeves are long enough for pants, but not big enough around, there's one solution, besides finding another sweater.

1. Make the pants, up to the point where the casing is made for the waistband.

2. Lay the pants flat and cut each side open.

3. Cut two strips of fabric, stretchy or otherwise, that match the side length of the pants. Make sure these strips are the same width and that they are wide enough to make the pants fit properly.

4. Sew the strips to each side of the pants front, right sides together.

5. Turn the pants inside out and sew the strips to the back face of the pants, right sides together.

6. Turn the pants right side out now and finish according to the instructions for making trousers.

Adult Sweater Too Short

If the sweater is too short for a dress, it may still work well as a long sweater top.

If, on the other hand, a dress or a long tunic top is essential, there are a few options available.

1. Use two sweaters for a dress. Cut a yoke-style top out of one sweater and create a fuller, gathered skirt out of another. It's a nice touch to use the sleeves from the sweater selected for the skirt to make the sleeves for the dress. This leaves the sleeves from the sweater that provided the yoke free to become pants or gaiters.

To do this, follow the instructions for the dress, but cut it off about 7 cm (3 inches) below the bottom of the armpit. Measure the length you need to complete the full dress length up from the bottom edge of the

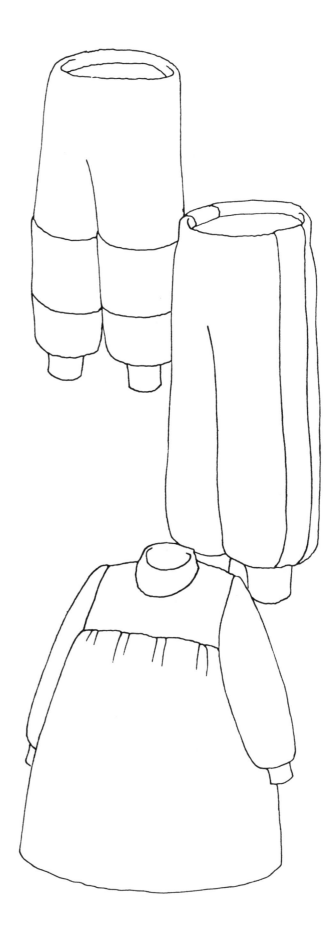

other sweater. Cut it and gather the raw edge to fit the yoke top. Sew the two, right sides together. Complete the outfit according to the instructions for making a top.

2. Still using another sweater, you might want to make a knitted ruffle to extend the hemline of the original sweater. This is easiest to do if you cut the finished edge off the bottom of another sweater. Cut this strip the width you want for your ruffle and gather the raw edge to attach to the bottom edge of the dress. This ensures that the bottom edge of the ruffle is a finished edge.

3. Cut a strip of another sweater (again) and cut the short dress off at the waistline. Sew the strip of the second sweater in at the waistline.

This solution offers the additional option of having the waist strip be wide and loose like the skirt of the dress, or a closer fit with a casing on the inside for an elastic as shown.

4. A final option for a sweater that's too short is to make it into a skirt. To do this, simply cut the sweater off (measuring up from the bottom, of course) at the desired skirt height plus 5 cm (2 inches) for a waistband. Finish the waistband as you would for trousers.

Adult Sweater Too Narrow

If the sweater to be transformed is long enough, but too narrow, there are a couple of simple options.

1. Before adding the sleeves or finishing the armholes, open up the sides of the finished dress or top. Then insert matching strips of another sweater or some other suitable fabric. Finish according to the instructions.

2. Before finishing the neckline, open up the centre front and the centre back of the top and insert strips of a suitable width and material. Then forge ahead with the rest of the instructions.

Alternative Sleeves and Armholes

1. A suggestion for getting everything out of one sweater is to forego pants in favour of gaiters. This way you only need the bottom two-thirds of the sleeve for the gaiters. The top one-third is quite full and would work extremely well for short puffy sleeves.

Finish the raw ends of the gaiters by applying a set of cuffs (store-bought or made from sweater scraps) that match or complement the sweater.

Finish the puffy sleeves by making a casing for .5-cm (¼-inch) elastic, cut to fit your child's upper arm. It's a good idea to cut this elastic a little on the loose side, because the upper arm is quite soft and sensitive.

3. To keep a knit armhole from stretching out too much, finish it with bright bias tape, store-bought or made from scraps. To keep a sleeve from stretching out at the armhole, try running piping in the seam between the sleeve and the armhole.

4. If you have any stretchy rib-knit that suits the sweater you've used, cut a length of it to fit the armhole. Cut this strip twice as wide as you want, plus about 2.5 cm (1 inch) for seam allowance. Sew the strip, right sides together, to form a loop. Fold the loop along its length and sew it, right sides together, to the armhole.

Alternative Necklines

1. If you're going to use any kind of a non-stretchy neckline, be sure it fits over the child's head.

2. You can, as mentioned earlier, use the neck off an old turtleneck to finish your top.

3. An interesting finish is to take the collar and enough of a shirt to include the first two buttons and apply it to your sweater top. The top couple of buttons need to be there, in most cases, to allow the finished garment to fit over the child's head.

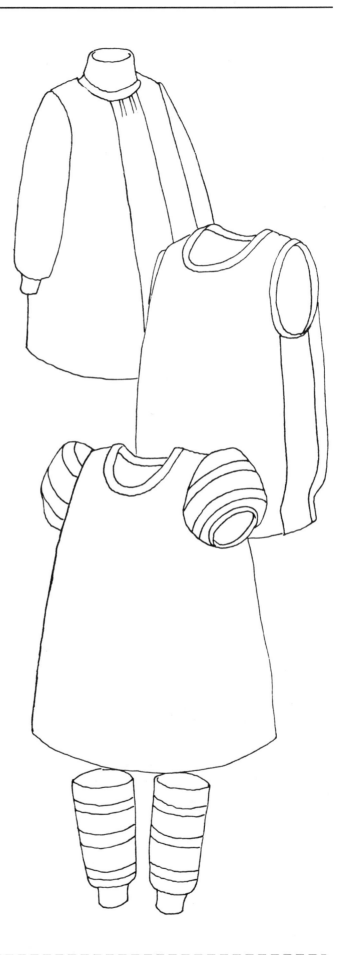

If you choose this finish, just cut the sweater neck large enough to fit the child's head without stretching. Then lay the sweater down with the shirt inside it. Trace the neck onto the shirt (with something that washes out) and then remove the sweater. Add a seam allowance to the traced neckline before cutting the collar out of the shirt. Turn the sweater inside out and place the shirt collar, right side out and up side down, inside the neck opening of the sweater. Make sure the shirt front has its right side to the front of the sweater before you sew the two together. Turn the sweater right side out again and run a line of stitching along the sweater edge of the neckline, being careful to fold the inside raw edge down. This will catch the raw edge in the topstitching and further secure the shirt collar. It looks more finished that way too.

If you've chosen this route, try using the shirt cuffs to finish the sweater sleeves, or full shirt sleeves to finish the top.

4. If there are enough long sweater scraps left, make a wide loop out of them. Fold this along its length and then gather it to apply to the neck as a knit ruffle. Make sure that this ruffle is either stretchy or fits over the child's head.

There's room for error with Short Kutz, *because, if you're resourceful and imaginative, your raw materials don't have to cost you anything. Make sure throughout, though, that you pace yourself, and leave plenty of room for fun and creativity.*

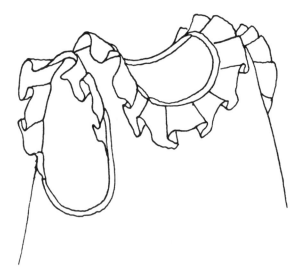

Sweaters to Jumpsuits and Bunting Bags

Designing and making
children's jumpsuits
and bunting bags
from adult sweaters

This information is more successfully applied with the use of a serger or an overlock stitch.

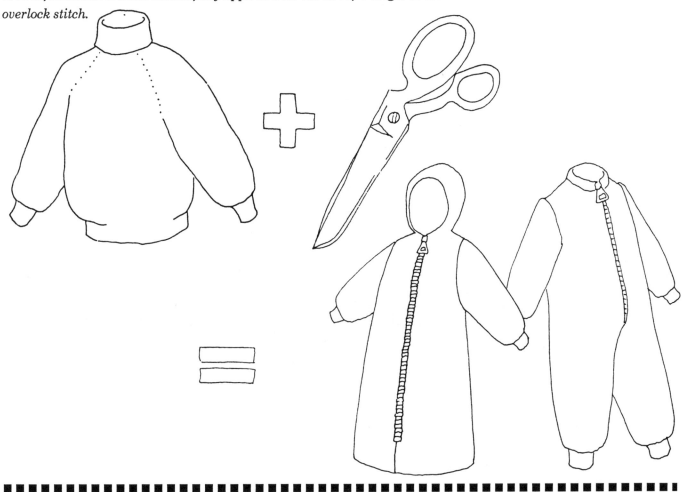

1. Measure

1. Measure your child according to the diagram.

2. If the child for whom you are sewing is unavailable, or your own child just won't cooperate, you can always check the dimensions on the back of an old pattern.

If the child you're sewing for is particularly long-limbed, you would be well advised to add about 5 cm (2 inches) to the sleeve and leg inseam measurements.

3. Measure the adult sweater to be sure that it's long enough to accommodate the child's full length. Measure from the neck to the toes for a bunting bag, to the ankles for a jumpsuit. If the neck of the adult sweater is not going to be used, measure from 5 to 8 cm (2 or 3 inches) below it.

4. If the adult sweater has a long cowl or turtleneck, it can be used to make a hood for the garment. Just measure the length of the neck to be sure it's long enough to accommodate the child's neck and head length.

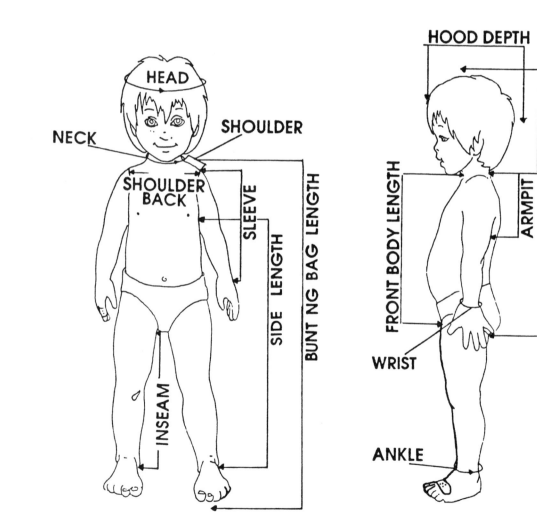

2. Mark

IF YOU'VE MADE A PATTERN *(see pages 118, 124)*

1. Place the sleeve pattern on the sleeve of the adult sweater. To use the original adult cuff, place the cuff end of the pattern along the bottom edge of the adult cuff. For a fuller sleeve, place the sleeve pattern at the shoulder end of the adult sleeve and cut off the cuff from the other end.

When you come to make your garment, gather the sleeve end to reattach it to the cuff. In this case, you can even reduce the size of the adult cuff by cutting off the original seam and restitching it before applying it.

Trace the sleeve pattern with dressmaker's chalk or any other washable marker.

Cut out the sleeves.

2. For a bunting bag, fold the sweater in half, front side out. Place the half front pattern piece of the bunting bag with the centre line along the centre fold of the sweater. If you're using the adult collar, place the shoulder of the pattern on the shoulder fold of the adult sweater. Trace the front pattern piece.

3. Open the sweater out and turn it over. Repeat step 2 using the back half pattern for the bunting bag. Be sure you mark the same side of the back as was marked on the front.

4. Cut as far as you've marked, *single thickness.*

5. Now carefully fold over the cut half of the bunting bag to the unmarked half of the adult sweater. This will enable you to use it as a pattern to cut the second side. *Remember to cut single thickness again.*

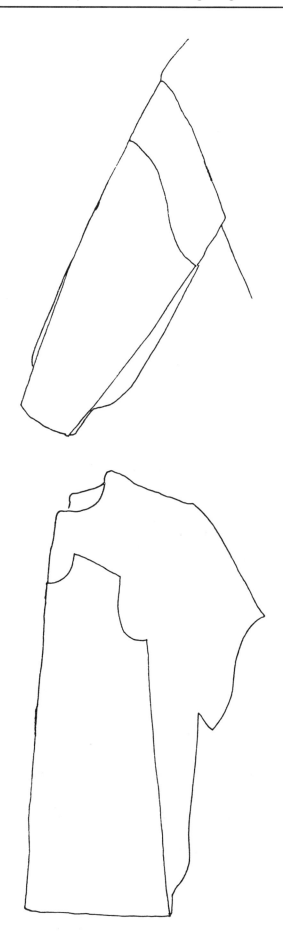

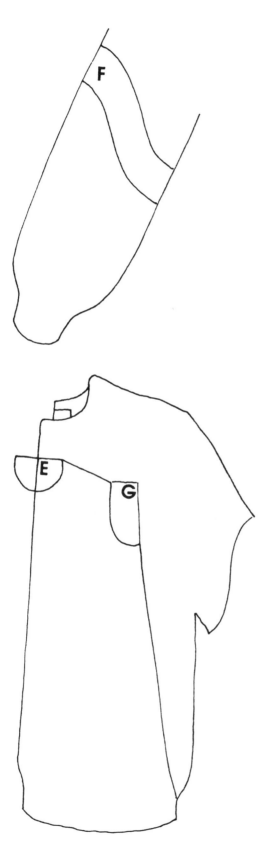

6. To make the jumpsuit, repeat steps 2 through 5 using the jumpsuit pattern.

✂ IF YOU HAVEN'T MADE A PATTERN

Select guides **A**, **B**, **E**, **F** and **G**.

Sleeves

1. Measure up from the cuff of the adult sleeve the desired sleeve length.

If the existing cuff is too loose, you may wish to cut it off to make it smaller. To do this, simply sew the cuff narrower. Reapply the cuff before you measure and mark your sleeve length. This will also give you a gathered sleeve.

2. Place the shoulder end of sleeve guide **F** at the desired sleeve length and trace the curve. Cut the sleeves *double thickness*.

Bunting Bag and Jumpsuit

1. Fold the sweater neatly in half lengthwise so that the front is showing. Carefully cut the sweater in half along the centre fold line.

2. Measure the child's full front length up the centre front line from the sweater bottom for a bunting bag.

3. For a bunting bag, place the back neck guide **E** at the top of this line, keeping the centre line of the guide on the centre line of the adult sweater. Trace the curve.

4. For a jumpsuit, measure up the cut centre line of the adult sweater from the bottom the desired inseam length and apply the front crotch guide **A** at this point. Trace the curve.

5. Extend the front crotch line up to the desired front body length and then apply the back neck guide **E** to the top of this line. Keep the centre line of the guide parallel to the centre fold of the sweater. Trace the curve.

6. From the top, or shoulder point of the neck curve, extend a straight line in a slight downward direction. Mark off the desired shoulder width plus 2.5 cm (1 inch) for seam allowance.

7. Place the armpit guide at the outside point of the shoulder line. (If the existing sweater neck is being used, measure out from the centre line half your desired shoulder back width. Place the armpit guide **G** at this point.)

8. Before tracing the armpit curve, make sure the guide is far enough out to accommodate more than one-quarter of the child's chest measurement.

9. Drop a line straight down to the outside bottom edge of the adult sweater for a bunting bag. Do the same for a jumpsuit with a full leg. If you wish a narrower leg for the jumpsuit, however, measure out from the inseam the width you desire at the cuff and extend and trace this line up to the side seam next to the bottom of the crotch.

10. Lay the sweater out flat and cut out the half that's marked. Be sure to cut *single thickness*.

11. Fold the cut half of the sweater front over on to the other half of the adult sweater front and use it as a pattern to cut the other half of the bunting bag or jumpsuit front. Once you've cut out this piece, however, with the two front halves still neatly lined up, take the front neck guide and place it over the back neck you've already cut to mark the front neck. Cut the new neck for the bunting bag or jumpsuit front *double thickness*.

12. Repeat steps 2 through 11 using the back length measurement and back neck guide for the bunting bag and the inseam and back body lengths with the back neck guide and the back crotch guide for the jumpsuit.

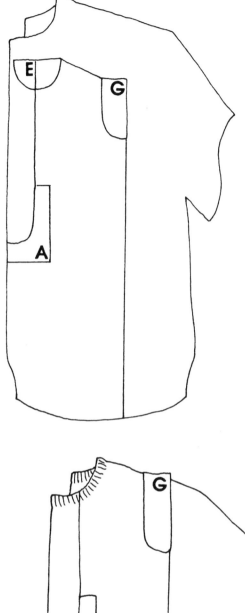

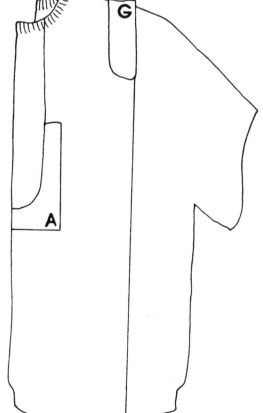

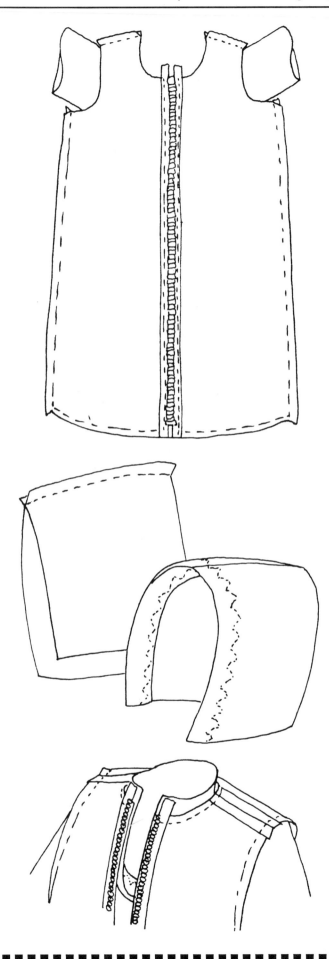

13. Find, or buy, a closed-end zipper to match either the front bunting bag length or the front body length of the jumpsuit you're creating. For a jumpsuit, if the zipper is too long it can be extremely uncomfortable, but if it's a little too short it can still work. For a bunting bag, if you use an open-ended zipper, the bunting bag can later be opened up at the bottom to make a robe.

3. Make

1. If you have a serger, serge the front centre edges of the bunting bag or jumper before sewing in the zipper. If you haven't got a serger or an overlock stitch on your machine, you'll have to apply seam binding to all your cut edges.

2. If you're not using the existing sweater neck, turn the sweater inside out and sew the shoulder seams.

3. Sew the side seams, the back seams and whatever part of the front seam is left below the zipper. Topstitch the zipper.

4. Insert the sleeves, right side out, into the inside-out sweater. Sometimes the sleeves may be a little large for the armholes. In this case, simply gather the sleeves enough at the shoulders to fit the armholes. If the sleeves are too small for the armholes, but fit the child nicely, narrow up the armholes a bit by dropping the shoulder seams down a bit.

5. Sew the inseam for the jumpsuit, or the bottom edge for the bunting bag.

6. If you're using an adult turtle or cowl neck for a hood, cut the tube off the neck. If the adult collar has a seam, cut it off instead of trying to pick it apart.

7. Fold the wide band that was the collar in half and sew one edge, as shown, right sides together. Finish the front edge of the hood. This can be done with bias tape, a strip of rib-knit or a stretch casing made from sweater scraps.

8. If you've made a casing of any kind, try a light elastic instead of a drawstring. Measure the elastic to fit loosely around the child's face and sew the ends in place before applying the hood to the garment.

9. Pin the front edges of the hood, right sides together, to the front edges of the neck. Pin the centre back seam of the hood, right sides together, to the centre back seam of the garment.

10. Sew the hood to the garment.

11. Make sure you've removed all the pins and then see if the outfit fits.

4. Notes

If you want to get a lot of mileage out of a bunting bag, start by making the hood extra big. Next, cut the sleeves 8 cm (3 inches) too long and finish the ends with a light drawstring threaded through the knit itself.

Use an open-ended zipper and cut the body of the bag perhaps 10 cm (4 inches) too long.

Finally, instead of sewing the end of the bag shut, sew a casing and thread through it a sturdy drawstring that ties at the bottom of the zipper. When your child is a toddler, you'll have a hooded robe just by removing the drawstrings from the bunting bag.

Adult Sweater Too Short

1. If the adult sweater is too short for a bunting bag, just make a warm little dress.

2. If it's too short for a jumpsuit, add cuffs to the legs of the jumpsuit. If this won't give you enough length, try adding a band of rib-knit or a strip cut from another sweater at the waist. This can be done either instead of cuffs or with cuffs. It all depends on the

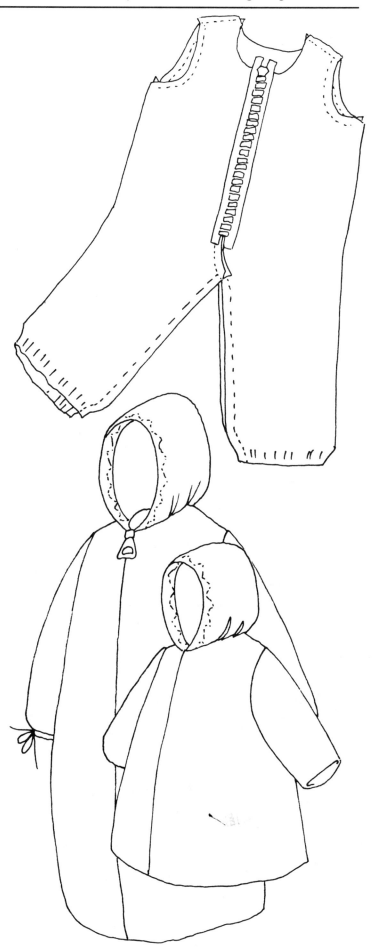

length of the adult sweater and the size of the child. If you're putting a band at waist level, do so before measuring for and applying a zipper.

3. Another way to lengthen a jumpsuit is to insert a band of some tougher fabric at the knees. Make sure, in this case, that the bands are the same width on each leg.

4. A suggestion for the jumpsuit, even if the legs aren't too short, is to apply knee and elbow patches made from a fairly sturdy, bright fabric. You might even want this fabric to be the same colour as the zipper. This will reduce wear and tear on the knit fabric and brighten up the garment at the same time.

Hood Hints

1. If you're going with elbow and knee patches to match your zipper, try a trim of the same colour in rib-knit or bias tape along the hood edge.

2. For a feminine touch, trim the hood with a knit or crocheted ruffle, or a length of gathered lace.

3. If you haven't got a turtle or cowl neck to work with, but you've got your heart set on a hood, work with two sweaters. Use the first sweater for the body and legs of the jumpuit.

From the second sweater, you get your sleeves. You can also use the body for a hood. Just measure a band of the sweater wide enough for the child's head and neck measurement, but twice as long as the desired hood depth. Use the rib-knit from the bottom edge of the sweater to finish the front edge of the hood. You'll have enough of this ribbing left over to make cuffs for the legs too.

And that's it. You're done! Hope you had fun.

CHAPTER TEN

Guides and Patternmaking

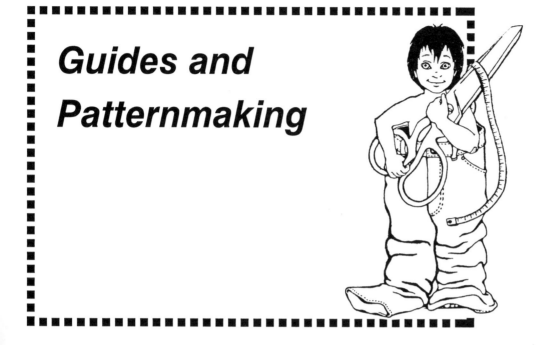

✂ THE SHORT KUTZ GUIDES

The guides or templates presented in this chapter are the key to *Short Kutz*. More traditional patterns provide you with the area to be cut out and sewn according to specific instructions, allowing very little room for innovation and imagination. *Short Kutz,* on the other hand, provides the means for outlining the pieces of the finished garment yourself. The instructions accompanying these guides enable you to design a garment specifically for your child's needs and shape.

The *Short Kutz* guides represent the curves necessary in a garment to accommodate things like necks, arms and legs. These curves need to be lengthened or shortened to fit the individual for whom you are sewing, but after that, it's simply a matter of placing the customized guides the right distance apart to fit the child and suit your design. Then you connect the curves with straight lines. With a little time and practice, you'll find yourself becoming a designer of some great clothes. You may find that you're having a lot of fun too.

Follow the directions laid out below for applying your child's measurements to the guides. Once the guides have been customized, they can serve two functions. They can either be used to make patterns or applied directly to old clothes to create a wide range of new, finished garments.

If you are making patterns, you may want to get a complete set of your child's measurements. Record the measurements on the size chart at the back of the book, and you are ready to make any of the pattern pieces contained in this chapter. ◀

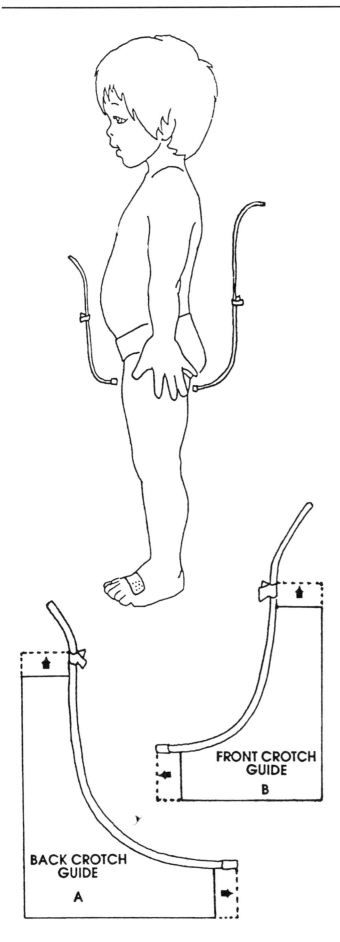

Crotch Guides A and B

If you are not fortunate enough to possess a flexible designer's curve, find yourself a piece of reasonably bendable wire, like a lightweight coat hanger opened out, and some masking tape. The wire should be at least 30 cm (12 inches) long, up to 76 cm (30 inches) for a larger child.

1. Dress the child in a pair of jeans or trousers that fit.

2. Place one end of the wire at the crotch point of the pants inseam (the pants on the child).

3. Keeping that end in place, carefully bend the wire around and up to match the curve of the child's bottom.

4. Wrap a piece of masking tape at the waist (on the wire).

5. Now place the back crotch guide **A** on a piece of paper large enough to allow for extensions and trace the outline.

6. Place the wire curve on the curve of the guide and extend (or shorten) the curve of the guide: out at the bottom to match the inseam point of the wire and up at the top to match the waist point on the wire.

7. Take the masking tape off the wire and repeat the entire process for the front crotch guide **B**.

8. Now cut out the new, customized crotch guides and label them clearly, including the child's name and age.

9. Repeat this information on an envelope, place the guides in the envelope and put it in a safe place.

Unless you have to dash out to pick up a child from school, or fish your two-year-old out of the toilet, it's time to move on to the armpit guides.

FRONT CROTCH
GUIDE

B

BACK CROTCH
GUIDE

A

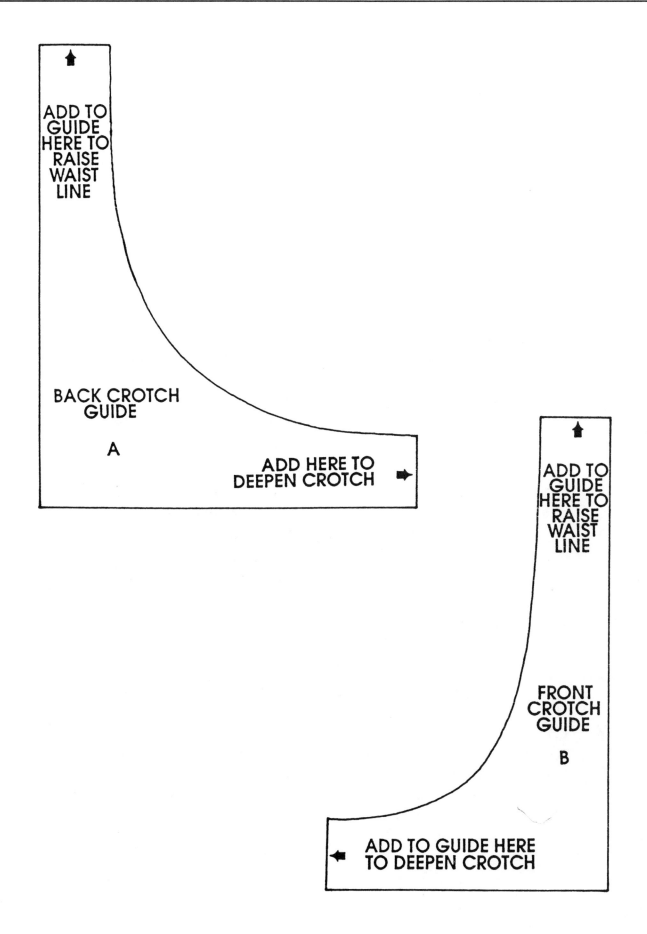

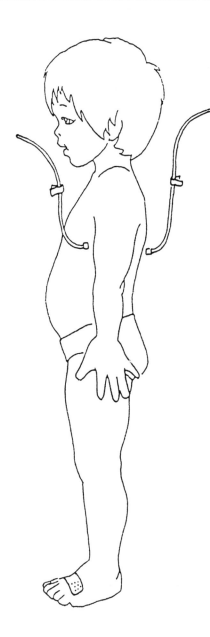

Overall Armpit Guides C and D

1. Dress your child in a sleeveless shirt that has side seams and find the armpit guides C and D.

2. If you have just used the wire to make the crotch guides, remove the masking tape. Place the end of the wire (carefully) at the side seam of the child's shirt at the desired side seam point for the overall armpit.

3. Now gently bend the wire around and up the back to the desired height for the back bib of the overalls.

4. Mark this point with the masking tape.

5. Trace the back armpit guide C onto a piece of paper or cardboard that's large enough to allow room for any necessary extensions.

6. Place the wire on the curve of the guide and draw an extension of this line to match the depth and height of the wire.

7. Remove the masking tape and repeat the process for the front armpit guide D. Cut out both customized armpit guides.

8. You now have a set of armpit guides to go with the crotch guides. Label them accordingly and place them in the same envelope.

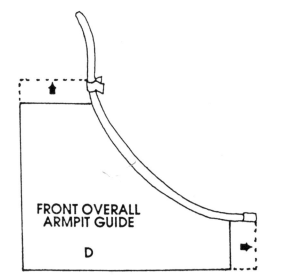

FRONT OVERALL
ARMPIT GUIDE

D

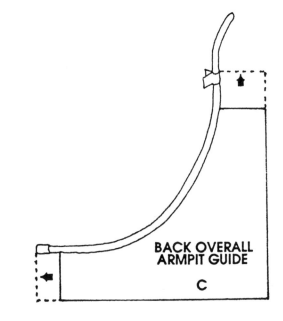

BACK OVERALL
ARMPIT GUIDE

C

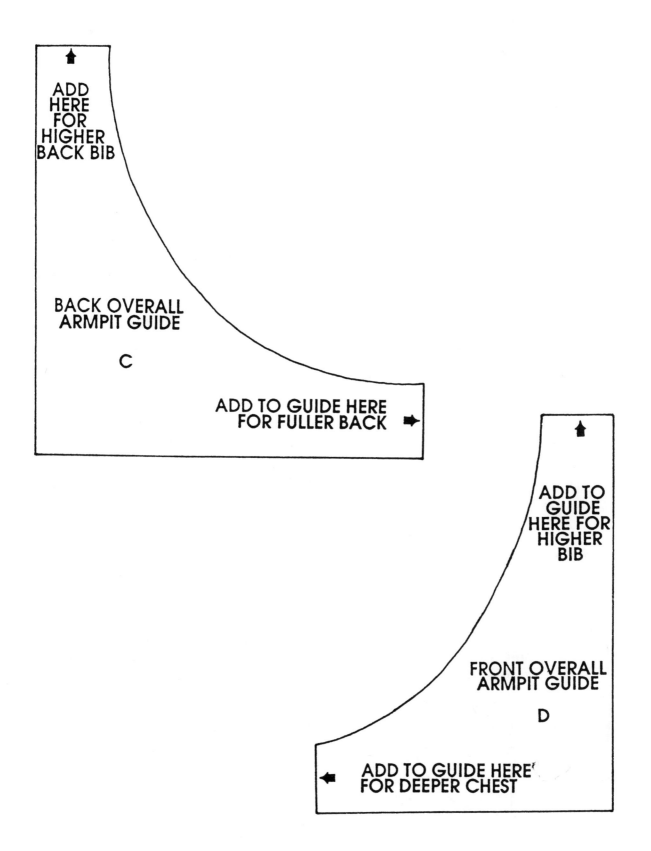

ADD HERE FOR HIGHER BACK BIB

BACK OVERALL ARMPIT GUIDE

C

ADD TO GUIDE HERE FOR FULLER BACK

ADD TO GUIDE HERE FOR HIGHER BIB

FRONT OVERALL ARMPIT GUIDE

D

ADD TO GUIDE HERE FOR DEEPER CHEST

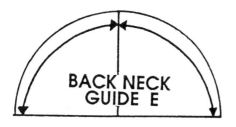

BACK NECK
GUIDE E

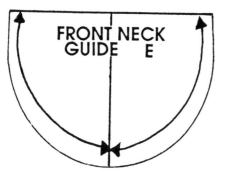

FRONT NECK
GUIDE   E

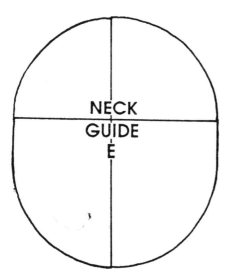

NECK
GUIDE
E

Neck Guide E

1. Add 5 to 8 cm (2 to 3 inches) to the child's neck measurement, 10 cm (4 inches) for an adult. Divide this number in two. Now take 5 cm (2 inches) from one half and add it to the second half. The smaller figure is the back collar measurement and the larger is the front collar measurement.

2. Divide the back collar measurement in half. From the midline in the neck guide, measure up the curve this amount and mark it. Do the same for the other half of the guide. Now trace the guide to these points on your cardboard and draw a straight line to connect the two top points.

3. Label this guide as the back neck guide and include your child's name and age.

4. Repeat step 2, but this time use the front collar measurement and label accordingly. Place them in the envelope as before.

Sleeve Guide F

1. Take a tape measure and place the zero end at the shoulder seam point on the child. Bring the rest of the tape around under the child's arm and back to the shoulder point to form a loop.

Make sure that this loop is loose enough to be a comfortable fit for an armhole. If it's too loose, it will be sloppy, but if it's too tight it will cut into the top of the child's arm.

2. Make a note of the measurement of the arm loop and divide it in half. Then divide it in half again.

3. Cut out the sleeve guide F.

4. There is a midline marked on the sleeve guide. Measure out, in both directions from this line, the final quarter measure. This will give you a centred sleeve width.

5. If the guide is too large for your child, cut it in half along the marked mid-line and trim it to fit, being sure to trim equal

amounts from the middle end of each half. Tape the trimmed halves back together at the new midline.

6. If the guide is too small, once again, cut it at the mid-point. Cut a strip of paper the same width as the guide and longer than you need to expand the guide as much as the child's measurement requires. Now mark the amount you wish to expand the guide in the middle of this strip, and tape the two guide pieces to the strip at either end of the marked section.

All this cutting and taping may sound like a lot of trouble, but if the guide is simply trimmed or extended at the ends, it could eliminate or exaggerate the curve of the original guide. In such a case the guide may not work properly anymore.

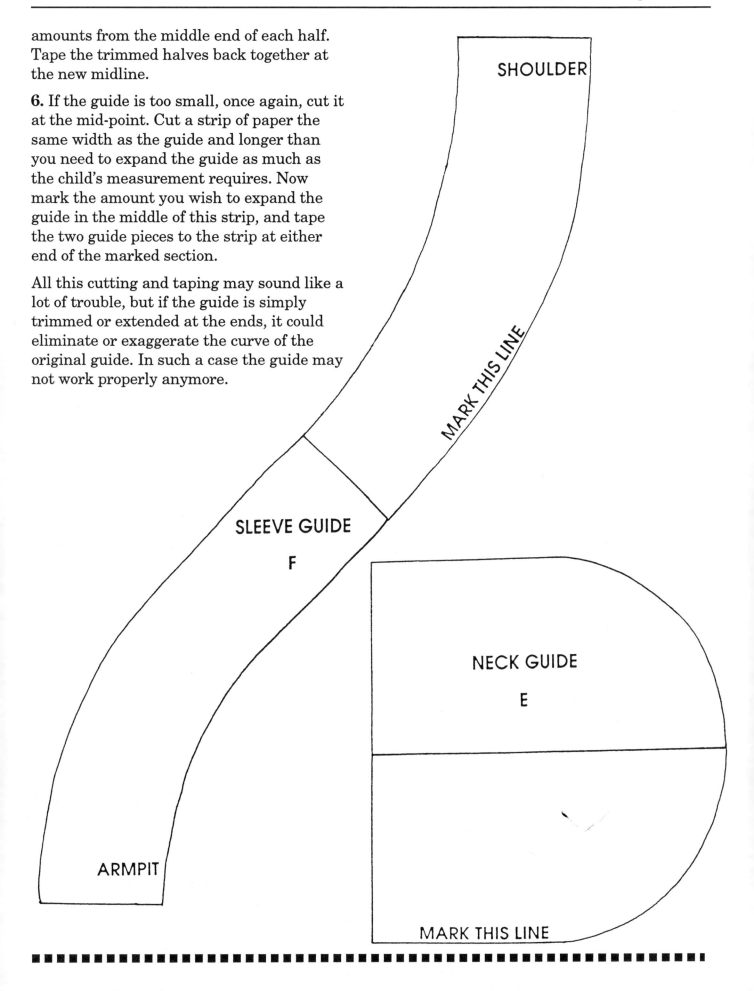

Armpit Guide G

1. Refer to the armpit measurement you used for the sleeve guide and apply it to the long, straight edge of armpit guide **G**. This is to ensure that the sleeve will fit the armhole when you make the finished garment. There is no need to adjust the width of the armpit guide, as you have applied the armpit measurement to the overall length of the guide. The completed shape of the armhole is created when you sew the shoulder seam of the garment.

2. If the guide is too long, cut it off at the straight end. If it is too short, tape on an extension or trace it onto cardboard and draw on the extension before cutting it out.

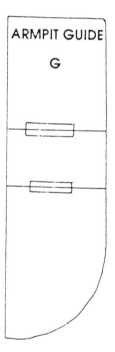

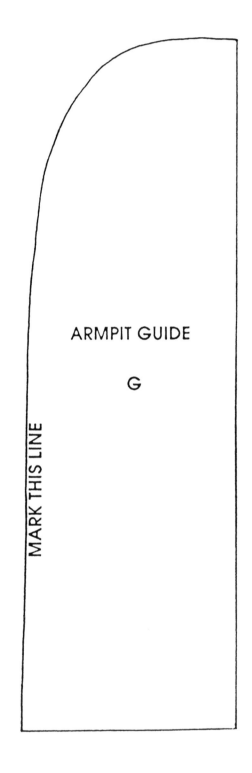

ARMPIT GUIDE

G

MARK THIS LINE

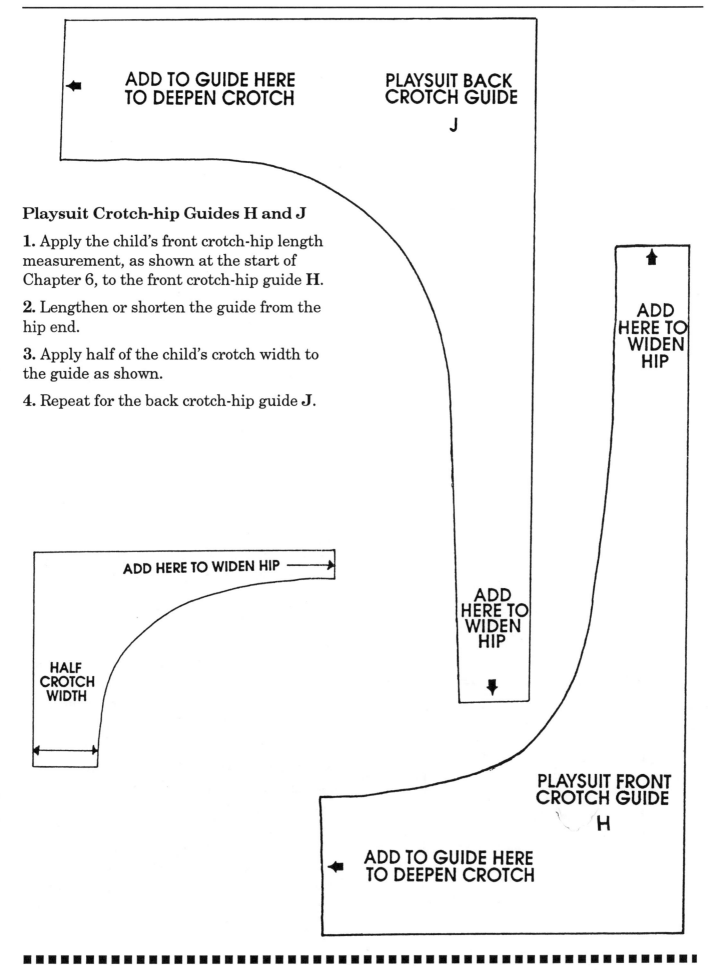

ADD TO GUIDE HERE
TO DEEPEN CROTCH

PLAYSUIT BACK
CROTCH GUIDE
J

Playsuit Crotch-hip Guides H and J

1. Apply the child's front crotch-hip length measurement, as shown at the start of Chapter 6, to the front crotch-hip guide **H**.

2. Lengthen or shorten the guide from the hip end.

3. Apply half of the child's crotch width to the guide as shown.

4. Repeat for the back crotch-hip guide **J**.

ADD
HERE TO
WIDEN
HIP

ADD HERE TO WIDEN HIP

HALF
CROTCH
WIDTH

ADD
HERE TO
WIDEN
HIP

PLAYSUIT FRONT
CROTCH GUIDE
H

ADD TO GUIDE HERE
TO DEEPEN CROTCH

✂ MAKING THE PATTERNS

If you have a staggering number of children or you plan on sewing kids' clothes for a living, you'd be well advised to make patterns from the guides you have created with this set of instructions. Patterns come in handy whether you simply hope to be very productive with your old clothes or plan to apply *Short Kutz* to new fabric as well.

Creating Pattern Paper

For pattern paper you have several options. Commercial pattern paper is available, but it's expensive and not always easy to find. Some kinds you can only order in bulk from a wholesaler. (Check the yellow pages for sewing equipment suppliers, or phone a community college for this information.)

Bristleboard or poster board, the kind that comes in many colours and lives in the school supply section of your drug store, is a good alternative. You may find, however, especially for children older than three or four, that you have to tape several sheets together. On the plus side, you can use a different colour for each child's patterns.

Butcher paper and shelf or banquet paper are other good choices, though not as sturdy. The totally budget-minded sewer, however, can lay open several brown, paper shopping bags and tape or glue them together. This works just fine and when you have no more use for the pattern, you can use it to start your fire in the morning.

Once you have selected or created your pattern paper, be sure the corners and edges are square, otherwise your pattern will end up being lopsided. You don't need special equipment to do this. Any large, square or rectangular book will do just fine. Simply place the corner of the book in the corners of your paper, one corner at a time. Line the sides of your paper up with the edges of your book. Sometimes a ruler helps with this. Repeat for all four corners. The result should be a perfect (well, almost) rectangle or square.

If you are creating your own pattern paper, don't feel that it has to be one enormous piece. It's often easier to work with several smaller pieces, one for each pattern. The pattern paper must be large enough, though, to accommodate the full height of the finished garment and there must be enough of it to allow room for the front, the back and sometimes the sleeves of the garment.

Overalls Pattern

Select crotch guides **A** and **B** and overall armpit guides **C** and **D**.

1. Measure up from the bottom left hand corner of the paper and mark your child's inseam length. Place the back crotch guide **A** at this point and trace the curve.

2. Extend the long line of the curve up the child's desired back length and mark this point clearly.

3. Measure across from this point and mark half of the desired back bib width plus about 2.5 cm (1 inch) for seam allowance. Mark this point.

4. Place the back overall armpit guide **C** at this point, with the curve facing in the opposite direction of the curve from the back crotch guide. (See illustration.)

5. Trace the guide, clearly showing where the bottom of the curve ends.

6. Place the front overall armpit guide **D** at this point so that the two armpit guides form a continuous U-shaped curve.

7. Now trace this curve.

8. Extend a line straight across from the top of your now complete armpit curve and measure off half of the desired front bib width plus about 2.5 cm (1 inch) for seam allowance.

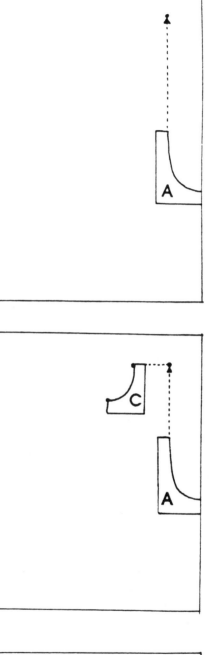

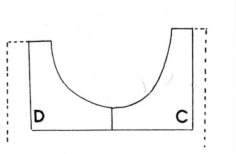

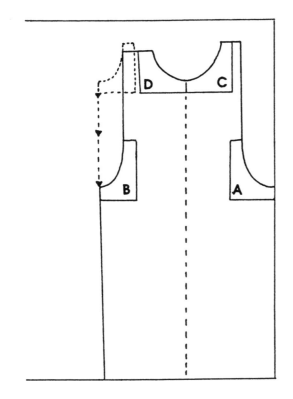

9. Mark this point clearly and place the top of the front crotch guide B at this point.

10. Now drop a line straight down from the outside point in the curve of this guide to the bottom edge of your paper.

11. Measure up this line from the bottom to the desired inseam height and clearly mark this point.

12. Move the front crotch guide **B** along this line to the marked inseam height and trace the curve. It should sweep up to join with the line you dropped from the bib.

13. Measure this extended curve line and make sure that it is fairly close to your child's desired front body length.

If your end product looks nothing like the diagram, or none of your pattern body lengths are even close to your child's size, relax and take a break before you try again.

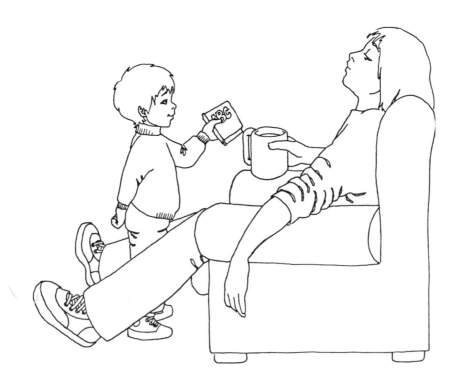

Pants Pattern

Select crotch guides **A** and **B**.

1. Measure up from the bottom right-hand corner your desired inseam height. Place the front crotch guide **B** here. (See illustration.)

2. Trace the curve and clearly mark the topmost point. Now extend the line beyond this point at least 5 cm (2 inches) for your waistband. Clearly mark this point.

3. Make a note on the pattern of the size of elastic you have allowed in the waistband measurement. This should be twice the width of the elastic plus 2 cm (¾ inch) for a casing hem and ease.

4. Measure left, from the top point marked, half of your child's waist measurement plus 5 to 8 cm (2 to 3 inches). This is to allow for seam allowance and movement, maybe even a little growth.

5. Mark this point clearly but do not trace the line yet.

6. Place the top of the back crotch guide A at this point, keeping the flat side parallel to the front crotch guide (and the side edge of the pattern paper).

7. Measure from the bottom point of the back crotch guide to the bottom edge of the pattern paper. This line must match the first inseam measurement as the two will eventually be sewn together to form one leg.

8. Slide the back crotch guide **A** up or down until the inseams match. Keep the guide in line with the waist point while you are doing this. This may be easier to do if you drop a line straight down from the waist point to the bottom edge of the pattern paper. This way you can simply measure up the line your desired inseam height and place your guide at this point.

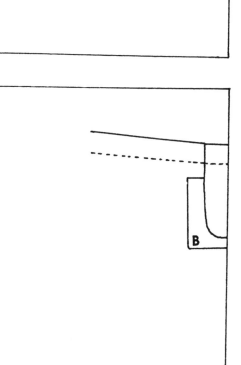

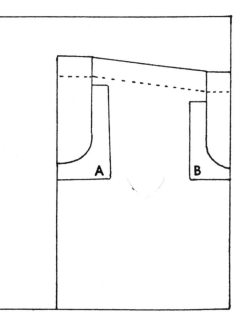

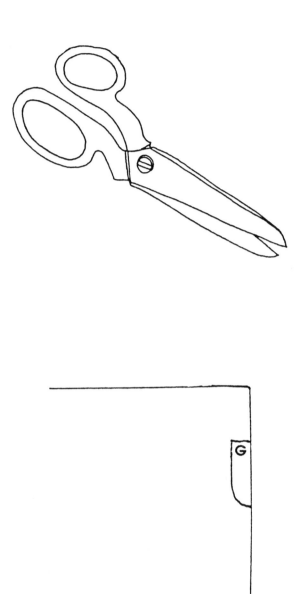

9. Once the guide is properly placed (see illustration), trace the curve. Remember to add the same amount to the top of the back crotch guide top as you did to the top of the front crotch guide for the waistband. Then draw a straight line connecting the top of both crotch curves. The dotted line in the diagram represents the desired fold line for the waistband casing.

10. Check the distance between the two crotch curves at waist height (the top) and the innermost point of the curve (the hip) to be sure that the resulting pants will fit your child. The pattern represents half the pants, so the waist and hip measurement must be greater than half the child's waist and hip measurement. Then cut out your pants pattern.

Jacket or Top Pattern

Select neck guide **E**, sleeve guide **F**, and armpit guide **G**.

1. Start with a piece of cardboard, paper or pattern paper that is large enough to accommodate your child's body length and at least two and a half times the body width.

2. Make sure, once again, that all the corners are squared (as opposed to rounded, ragged or angled).

3. Measure up from the bottom right-hand corner the desired side body length and mark this point.

4. Place the bottom point of armpit guide **G** at this point with the straight side of the guide going up along the straight edge of the paper.

 5. Trace the guide, being sure to clearly mark the top point of the curve.

6. If you aren't comfortable merely eyeballing the shoulder angle, drop a line straight down from the top of the armpit curve to the straight bottom edge of the paper.

7. Measure this line and add about 2.5 cm (1 inch), more for a child older than three or four. Mark this new measurement approximately where the neck point of the shoulder seam will be.

8. Measure your desired shoulder (as in shoulder to neck) width, plus 2.5 cm (1 inch) for seam allowance, across from the top of the armpit curve and bring it up to match the height of the mark you made in step 7.

9. Now draw a line connecting the top armpit point and this new point. This represents the shoulder of your front jacket pattern.

10. Place your front neck guide **E** at the neck end of the shoulder line you just drew, keeping the midpoint line on the guide parallel to the side of your paper.

11. Now trace the curve from the shoulder point to the midpoint on the guide.

12. Drop a line straight down to the bottom of the paper, keeping it parallel to the edge of the paper, and voilà, you have half your jacket front.

13. Measure this last line, by the way, in order to know what length of open-ended zipper to buy for your jacket.

14. To be on the safe side, measure the width of the above pattern piece just below the armpit curve to be sure that it is 5 cm (2 inches) bigger than one-quarter of your child's upper chest measurement. For a jacket pattern, allow even more extra room through the chest. If it's too small, after you cut out the pattern merely add to the side and front by taping on strips of paper that are the appropriate width.

15. When you've cut out this first pattern piece, flip it over and trace its mirror image. This will give you the patterns for both halves of the jacket front.

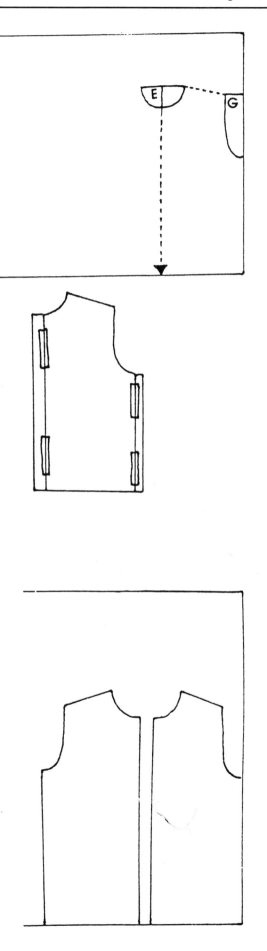

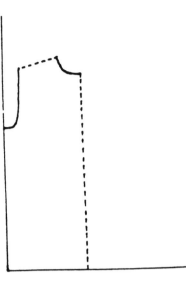

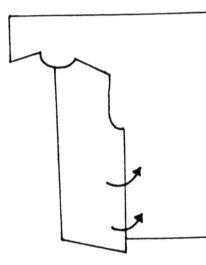

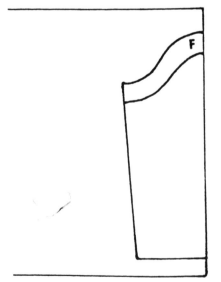

16. To make your jacket or top back, repeat steps 3 to 15, but use the back neck guide instead of the front neck guide and don't cut the first half at the centre line. Simply fold the first half over and trace it, so the back is one pattern piece.

Sleeve Pattern

Select sleeve guide **F**.

1 . Place the flat edge of the shoulder end of sleeve guide **F** against a straight edge of your paper. (See illustration.)

2. Measure from the shoulder line, along the straight edge, your desired sleeve length plus about 8 cm (3 inches). Mark this point.

3. Draw a line out from the edge at 90 degrees here and mark it off equal to your child's wrist measurement less 2.5 to 5 cm (1 to 2 inches). Remember that the pattern piece you're making represents half of the sleeve. For a fuller sleeve, add 5 to 8 cm (2 to 3 inches).

4. Draw a line from the end of this wrist line straight back up to the armpit end of the sleeve guide. You now have a sleeve pattern that represents half of a sleeve. Cut it out.

5. Trace this piece flipped over and you will have two half-sleeves.

6. Remember to label all your pattern pieces.

7. If you'd rather work with a full sleeve pattern, tape the two you've made back to back and trace them again as one. (See illustration.) You now have two full sleeve patterns or 4 halves.

Jumper, Dress, Tunic or Coat Pattern

Select neck guide **E**, sleeve guide **F**, and armpit guide **G**.

1. Measure up the right side of your pattern paper, from the bottom right-hand corner, the desired side length, hem to armpit, of the garment.

2. Mark this point and then measure in at a right-angle .5 to 8 cm (2 or 3 inches). A big book will come in handy here too.

3. Drop a line down from this point to the outside, right-hand, bottom corner. This line represents the side of the garment, so you can move the top point in or out to achieve the fullness you desire in the finished garment. For a fuller skirt, merely measure in farther than .5 to 8 cm (2 or 3 inches) at the top point. (See illustration.) For a gentler angle, measure in less.

4. Once you have established the side angle for your garment, place the bottom point of the armpit guide **G** at the top of this line. Be sure to keep the flat side of the armpit guide parallel with the side of the pattern paper.

5. Trace the curve of the armpit guide, clearly marking the top point.

6. Measure and draw a line across from this point your desired shoulder width plus 2.5 cm (1 inch) for seam allowance. Angle this line upward 2.5 to 5 cm (1 or 2 inches) when you draw it. (See illustration.)

7. At the inside or top end of this shoulder line place the upper point of the front neck guide **E**. Be careful to keep the centre line in this guide parallel with the side of the pattern paper.

8. Trace the front neck guide curve to the midpoint.

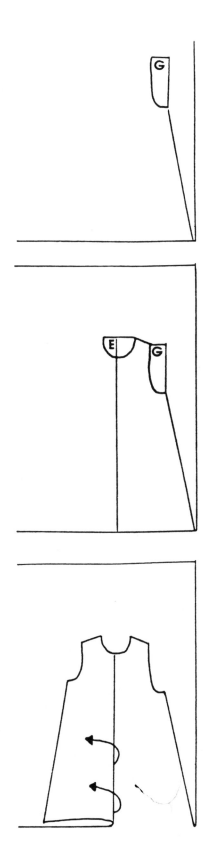

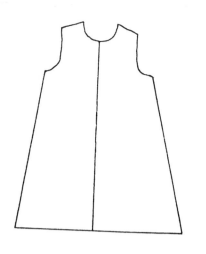

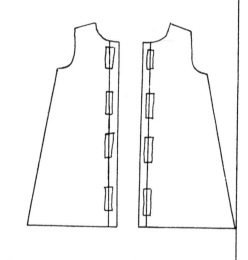

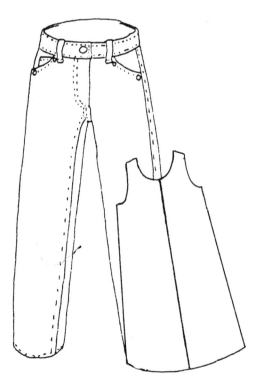

9. It's very important to have both sides of a pattern piece match, so rather than repeat all the steps you've just made, cut what you've traced and fold it over. Be sure to fold the shoulder point over to the same height for the second half.

10. Now use the cut half of the pattern as a guide to trace the rest of the pattern front.

11. Draw a line down the centre of the pattern piece.

12. To make the back pattern, go to the bottom left-hand corner of your paper and repeat steps 1 through 11. This time, however, use the back neck guide.

13. To be on the safe side, at this point check your measurements against the pattern, to be sure it will fit the child you had in mind. When you're finished you will have two pattern pieces: one for the front and one for the back. Make sure the side seams are all the same length.

14. If you want the option of a front- or back-opening garment, simply cut the front or back pattern pieces into two equal halves, using the lines you drew up the centres. Then tape a strip 2.5 cm (1 inch) wide to each centre line of the patterns for seam allowance and cut two strips 8 cm (3 inches) wide for front plaquets and two 4 (1½-inch) strips for interfacings.

15. Cutting the patterns in half, up the centre line, even if you aren't applying buttons or a zipper, makes them easier to apply to jeans, as you can place the entire pattern half directly on the pant leg without worrying about the location of the centre line. The edge of the pattern centre can be placed along the selected edge of the pant leg.

If you're making a coat, or a dress with sleeves, go to page 118 for instructions on making the sleeve pattern.

16. For the jumper, if you're feeling really ambitious and the kids won't be home from school or up from their naps for a while yet, try using the armpit guides **C** and **D** instead of armpit guide **G** to make a bib-top jumper pattern. For a fastenable-strap jumper pattern, simply extend the front shoulder pieces about 4 cm (1 1/2 inches). Extend the shoulders on the jumper back pattern about 8 cm (3 inches). For a particularly nice finish, round the corners of these strap ends.

If your children have been cooperative and the phone quiet, you may now very well have three custom-designed jumper patterns.

Congratulations! If the children are still either not present or self-entertained, take a break. You've earned it.

17. Now, just to be on the safe side, go back to all your patterns and measure them across just below the armpit. Will they fit the child for whom they were designed? Remember, if the garment is to be a pull-on, it must be several centimetres (a few inches) larger around than the child's chest.

18. If it's too close to the child's chest measurement, you may be able to save the the garment by putting a zipper in at the front or back.

19. Check the front and back centre lines to be sure the back is slightly longer than the front so that the garment will hang right. Both need to be longer than the sides, unless you're working with an extremely low, scooped neck. Check the side lengths of your patterns to make sure they match.

20. Finally, if you or your children are really fussy, when you're laying out your pattern, add 2.5 to 5 cm (1 or 2 inches) to the side length. This will leave you enough room to measure your desired front and back centre lengths as well and connect them to the side lengths with a gently curved line. If you are

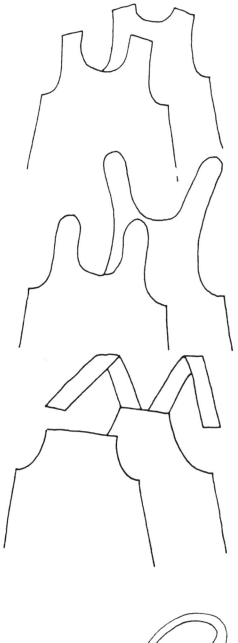

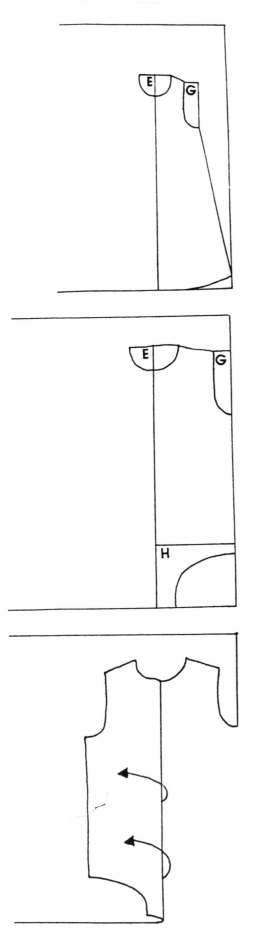

trying to design a very full garment, you will have to do this anyway, in order to have it hang right.

To make the curve of the hem a little easier to draw, try tracing the curve from another finished jumper or dress that fits fairly well and hangs nicely.

Rompers and Sunsuit Pattern

Select neck guide **E**, sleeve guide **F**, armpit guide **G**, and crotch-hip guides **H** and **J**.

1. Measure up from the bottom right-hand corner your desired side body length measurement plus 15 cm (6 inches). Mark this point.

2. Place the point of the armpit guide **G** at this mark, with the flat edge running up along the straight edge of the paper.

3. Trace the curve.

4. From the top point of the armpit curve, measure across and up at a slight angle, the desired shoulder width plus 2.5 cm (1 inch) for seam allowance. Mark this point and draw the line connecting it with the top of the armpit curve.

5. Place the front neck guide **E** at the inside point of the shoulder line. Keep the centre line of the neck guide parallel with the side of the paper.

6. Trace the curve of the neck guide to the midpoint.

7. Drop a line straight down from the centre line of the neck guide. This line must be parallel with the side of the paper as well.

8. Measure down this centre line your desired front body length and add 5 to 8 cm (2 or 3 inches), depending on the size of the child. For a child over six you may want to add another 2.5 cm (1 inch).

9. Measure down from the bottom of the armpit curve your desired side body length and add about 5 cm (2 inches). Mark this point.

10. Place the centre of the front crotch guide **H** at the base of the centre line and angle the end towards the side point marked in step 9.

11. Trace the curve.

12. All going well, you now have one-half of the front romper or sunsuit pattern.

13. Rather than repeat all the steps you have taken so far, cut the half of the pattern that you've made (except for the centre line).

14. Fold over the cut half of the pattern along the centre line and trace it out for the other half of the pattern.

15. Repeat steps 1 through 14, measuring up from the bottom left corner, using the back neck guide **E** and crotch guide **J**. This will give you your pattern back.

16. If you are making a romper with sleeves, refer to page 118 for instructions.

17. In the case of a sunsuit, where there's no need for sleeves, it's very effective to cut a much fuller neck and extend the shoulders up into rounded, fastenable straps.

To do this, simply cut the neck guides up the centre line and spread them apart to achieve the desired neck width. Make sure the resulting, wider back and front guides are the same width.

Add about 4 cm (1 ½ inches) to the length of the front shoulder and about 8 cm (3 inches) to the length of the back shoulder and round the ends.

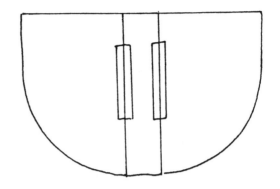

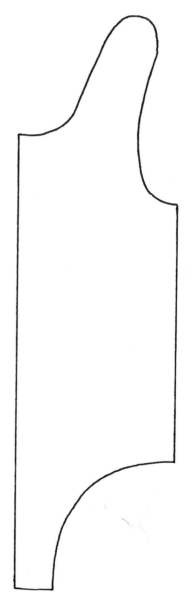

Jumpsuit or Bunting Bag Pattern

Select crotch guides **A** and **B**, neck guide **E**, sleeve guide **F**, and armpit guide **G**.

1. Measure up from the bottom right-hand corner of the paper the desired full side body length. If the jumpsuit is to have cuffs, go 5 cm (2 inches) beyond the ankle point.

For a bunting bag, extend the measurement 8 to 10 cm (3 or 4 inches) beyond the child's feet— more if the bag is to fit for longer than a couple of months. Remember that tiny babies grow at a tremendous rate.

2. At the top of the side body measurement, on the edge of the paper, place your armpit guide **G**.

3. Trace the curve.

4. From the top of the armpit curve, draw a line to the left and slightly upward. Measure along this line and mark the desired shoulder width, plus 2.5 cm (1 inch) for seam allowance.

5. Place the front neck guide **E** at the inside end of the shoulder line. Keep the centre line of the guide parallel with the side of the pattern paper.

6. Trace the curve of the guide as far as the centre line.

7. If you're making a jumpsuit, jump to step 11.

8. For a bunting bag, go 2.5 cm (1 inch) past the midpoint of the neck curve before marking the centre point. This space is added to provide seam allowance for a zipper down the front of the bunting bag. Drop a line straight down from this centre point to the bottom of the pattern paper. Make sure this line is parallel to the edge of the paper.

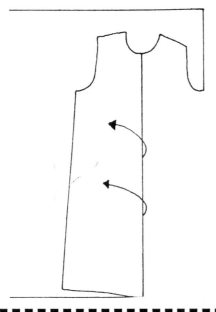

9. To make the other half of the front bunting bag, cut the first half out, flip it and trace it. Then cut out the second half.

10. To make the back pieces, repeat steps 2 through 9, using the back body length and the back neck guide. Don't add 2.5 cm (1 inch) to the neck measurement, though, because there's no zipper going in the back.

11. If you're making a jumpsuit, measure down from the centre point on the front neck curve your desired front body length.

12. Place the front crotch guide **B** at the bottom of this line.

13. Trace the curve.

14. Drop a line straight down from the bottom end of the crotch guide **B** to the bottom edge of the pattern paper. Keep this line parallel with the side of the paper. Now cut out the pattern. This piece represents half of the garment front. In order to have both halves, simply flip the first half, trace it, and cut it out.

15. For the jumpsuit back, repeat steps 11 through 14, using the back body measurement and the back crotch guide **A**.

There may be many more patterns that can be created with the guides in this chapter. The more you use the *Short Kutz* system the more readily you will be able to apply your own imagination. *Short Kutz* is just a starting point. Try the different ideas laid out in the preceding chapters and then experiment to your heart's delight.

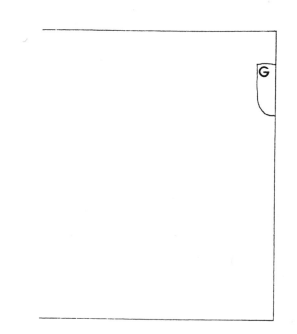

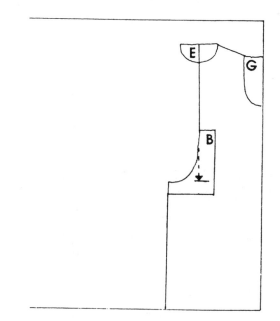

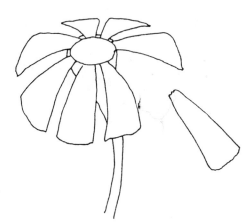

CHAPTER ELEVEN

Cheap
Kutz

This chapter is devoted to helping you cut even more corners when you design and sew for your kids (or anyone else's too . . .).

Everyone has a collection of *stuff* in their homes that they're hoping will fit or be in style again someday. Then there's all the *stuff* you've been saving to give to a local charity or your cousin. There's also the bag of *stuff* your cousin gave to you last year. And it's with the bag of *stuff* that you're mother gave to you the year before that. Or was it two years before that? Finally, there's all the *stuff* in everyone else's closet in the house. If you've never saved anything like this in your life, there's always the local thrift store or your mother's basement.

Now, make a big pot of tea or coffee, clear some floor space and roll up your sleeves. (If you're feeling really brave, invite your kids to help sort. Remember, though, that they may want to keep half the *stuff* as priceless treasures.)

Shoes

1. Old shoes by themselves are useful as shoes if you can still wear them. Otherwise, they can be fun in a dress-up box.

2. They're also a source of things like laces, buckles, bows and straps.

3. The tongues from an old pair of high-top runners can become a pair of rabbit's ears or droopy hound dog's ears. Short runner tongues can be bear's ears. These creatures can be stuffed toys, appliqués on the bibs of overalls or jumper fronts, or part of Hallowe'en costumes.

4. Laces can be used to make a drawstring on sleeve ends or across a pocket top. Long laces can even fit into the casing on a jacket bottom.

5. Velcro straps can be used on the front of overalls, or even a jacket front. Just remember to pick out the loops or D rings the straps go through as well.

6. Try a little bit of life on the wild side. Cut the heel and sole off a pair of canvas runners and sew what's left onto the thighs of a pair of pants or overalls as lace-up pockets!

7. Take the cuffs from a pair of high-tops, use ¼-inch (.5-cm) elastic instead of laces, and sew them on as jacket or pant cuffs.

8. Try high-cut tops to finish the front ends of a collar on a jacket. Add fluorescent laces and you've got a great finish.

Slippers

1. Remember the fuzzy-toed slippers that had no heel and sort of fwapped your heels as you walked? If you cut the rubber sole off, the tops are a perfect shape and size for a little pocket on a jumper or overalls. With a little bit of extra effort, some buttons and scraps of fleece or felt, each pocket could be a little face. Don't forget the tongues from your old sneakers for ears.

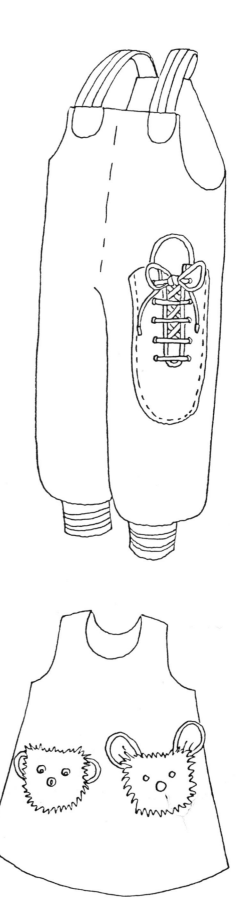

2. Some knit slippers wear out on the bottom long before the ribbed cuffs have even begun to stretch out or fall apart. These cuffs are great for finishing off pants and sweater tops or replacing worn cuffs on jackets.

3. You may find an old pair of slippers that have a knee-high knit top to them. If you cut off the worn-out foot, you can sew on the cuffs from the other old slippers or an old sweater and produce a pair of gaiters.

Socks

1. Most of the time, the only part of a sock that wears out is the foot. This leaves you with a veritable gold mine of cuffing for all your sewing projects.

2. Knee socks are good for sweater sleeves. You can also cut them open lengthwise and resew them together to make a single, fatter tube. Folded over on itself this tube becomes a great turtleneck.

3. An old pair of cross-country socks can be treated like adult sweater sleeves and turned into a small child's pants (see Chapter 8).

4. A pair of short sock cuffs, cut open and then cut in a U shape, make great little pockets too.

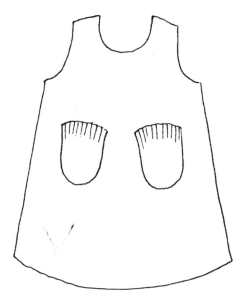

5. All the odd socks left over by your dryer should be saved for a rainy day. They're a great starting point for hand puppets. Fold the sock flat on its side and cut in from the toe (see illustration). Then cut an oval to fit the opened-out toe from some other old scraps. Sew it in with teeth and a tongue. Make wool pompoms for googly eyes and you've got a hand puppet. Here's where your running shoe tongues might come in handy for ears again.

6. A really quick trick with an old sock is to stuff a tennis ball in the end. A child can stand, backed up against a wall, and bang this back and forth for quite a while. It's also a good toy or game in an area where you have to deal with a lot of traffic. The ball can't get away very easily.

Slips and Nighties, Bras, Briefs and Boxers

1. Slips and nighties, old camisoles or teddies are all a tremendous source of lace, little buttons, snaps and hooks, and wonderfully soft material for linings.

2. You can also use the satiny fabrics, cut in strips, for very comfortable bias tape. If you don't have a serger and you want to work with old sweaters, you can use this bias tape to finish all the seams so that they're soft and unfrayable.

3. The satin spaghetti straps from some old slips and nighties work well as drawstrings in the cuffs of babies' sweater tops and pants.

4. The lace in these old garments runs from cotton eyelet to fine, almost antique lace. It can be applied at cuffs, collars, hems, pocket tops, yoke bottoms and anywhere else you need a little feminine touch.

5. You can save the fabric from really wild boxer shorts, but the best thing to pinch from old briefs and boxers is elastic. Even if it looks pretty ratty, if there's any stretch left, save it. You can cover it in a bright casing for shoulder straps and waist bands.

2. The same applies to the strapping from old bras.

3. A real find is an old pair of stretch ski pants. They're a great source of stretchy side panels.

Shoulder Pads

1. All those over-sized, out-of-date shoulder pads can be stuffed into old socks or sewn

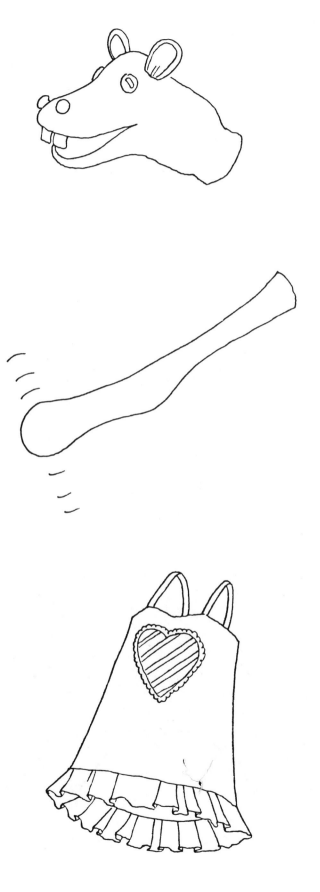

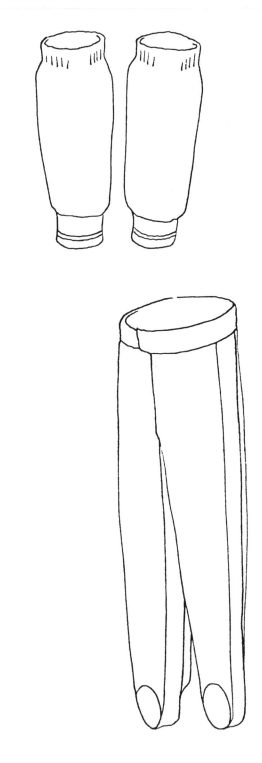

into a custom-made doll shape to make a wonderfull, soft puppet or doll.

2. They also work well inside knee and elbow patches as padding for an active child.

3. Use them in the appliqué on an activity blanket for a baby.

4. Cover the shoulder pads in the pile lining scraps from an old coat for a pair of earmuffs. Then make an elastic headband with an old piece of waistband elastic covered in a bright casing. Put the headband on the child to figure the placement for the earmuffs and sew them on. Use satin strapping or shoelaces for ties to go under the chin. Once again, a little imagination and bits of buttons and yarn could give each earmuff a little face.

Curtains,Sheets, Dresses, Etcetera

If you look around with an eye for fabric as opposed to finished garment, you may find a fortune in raw materials lurking in your home.

1. When a shirt has worn out at elbows, collar and cuffs, the material on the back is often good as new. There's also plenty there, depending on the size of the shirt, for overall and jumper facings, a small summer dress or plenty of bias tape.

2. An old pair of jeans that aren't worth mending any more may still have a fair amount of sturdy denim left on the backs of the legs and under the pockets. You may need two pairs of jeans in this state to make a pair of overalls or a jumper, but the material is still sound, so why waste it?

3. Then you have all the zippers, buttons, snaps, hooks, buckles and straps off any old clothes. Not to mention the lace, piping, elastic and rick-rack.

4. Use ready-made pockets picked off any garment to finish a child's clothes.

Blankets and Quilts

1. Often a blanket or quilt will be discarded because it's torn, worn or tattered in a few spots. As a bed covering it's finished. Look again, though, and you'll discover many metres of wool or quilted fabric for baby blankets, bunting bags, jacket linings or even snow-suit linings.

2. A really tattered quilt can still be turned into several tea cozies at Christmas time, or even slippers. Lay a sock flat on its side on the quilt. Trace the sock, adding about 5 cm (2 inches) seam allowance all around. Cut this out and flip it to use as a pattern for the other half of the first slipper. Take the first two pieces and place them again on the quilt, right sides together. Cut out the two halves of the other slipper now.

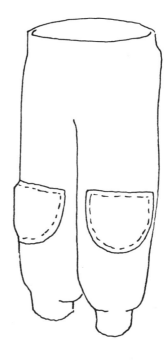

Trace the sole of a shoe that's the right size. Add a 1.5 cm (½ inch) for a seam allowance and cut it out then flip to cut the sole of the other foot. Sew the top left half of each slipper to the top right half of each slipper, right sides together. Attach the soles, being careful to line up the centre of the sole with the centre seams of the slipper tops. If the tops are too large, gather them at the toe. If the tops are too small, add a strip up the front of each top and then attach the soles.

3. Often the only thing of use from the quilt is the stuffing, loosely contained by shreds of fabric. Re-cover this with bright curtain material or an old summer dress, to create a delightful, bright lining for a denim jacket or vest.

4. The same applies to old quilted house-coats and jacket linings.

Sort through your stuff carefully. Don't think of what it is or has been, but see it instead as free raw materials. Then try to think of what it could be.

Be careful though, your imagination may run away with you. And don't forget to have fun.

Family Size Chart

Measure your child (or children) according to the diagrams and record the measurements on the following chart. To keep records for all your family members, just photocopy the chart. If you keep the charts over a number of years, you will have an interesting record of your child's growth.

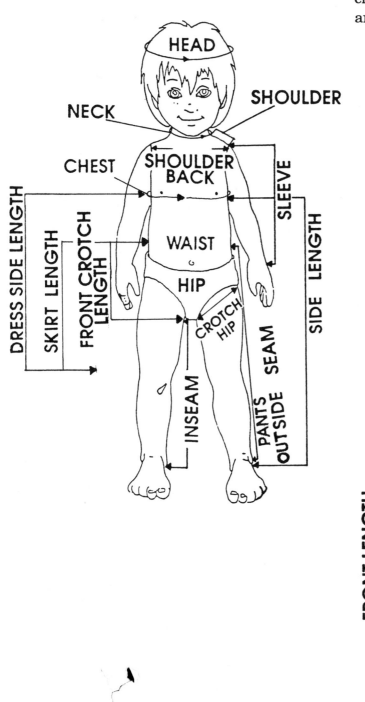

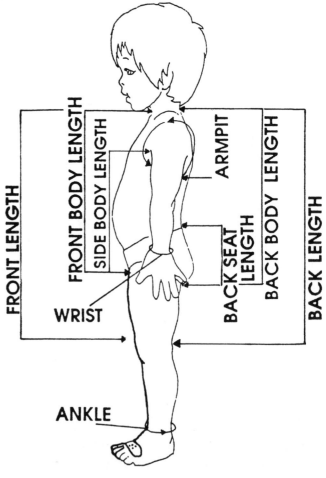

CHILD'S NAME   **YEAR**

HEAD				
NECK				
SHOULDER				
SHOULDER BACK				
ARMPIT				
BACK LENGTH				
BODY BACK LENGTH				
BACK SEAT				
FRONT LENGTH				
FRONT BODY LENGTH				
FRONT CROTCH LENGTH				
SLEEVE				
WRIST				
SIDE LENGTH				
SIDE BODY				
CHEST				
WAIST				
PANTS OUTSIDE SEAM				
INSEAM				
DRESS SIDE LENGTH				
SKIRT LENGTH				
HIP				
ANKLE				
HEIGHT				
WEIGHT				
SHOE SIZE				

About the Author

Melanie Graham is an active mother of three—Jamie, Katey, and Toby—who well knows the value of the few hours and minutes gleaned from a busy parent's day. Her *ShortKutz* sewing method evolved from her involvement in an outdoor clothing manfacturing business and her interest in producing attractive children's clothing—clothing that could be made quickly and easily by a parent with limited time. Over the years she has taught numerous workshops featuring her original designs, now compiled in *ShortKutz*.